Fun Learning Activities For Modern Foreign Languages

Jake Hunton

Illustrations by Les Evans

Crown House Publishing Limited
www.crownhouse.co.uk

First published by
Crown House Publishing Ltd
Crown Buildings, Bancyfelin, Carmarthen, Wales, SA33 5ND, UK
www.crownhouse.co.uk

and

Crown House Publishing Company LLC
PO Box 2223, Williston, VT 05495, USA
www.crownhousepublishing.com

First published 2015. Reprinted 2017, 2018.

British Library of Cataloguing-in-Publication Data

A catalogue entry for this book is available from the British Library.

Print ISBN: 978-184590892-8
Mobi ISBN: 978-184590956-7
ePub ISBN: 978-184590957-4
ePDF ISBN: 978-184590958-1
LCCN: 2014958177

Edited by Peter Young

Printed and bound in the UK by TJ International, Padstow, Cornwall

Foreword

by Sir Christopher Stone, Chief Executive, The Arthur Terry Learning Partnership

This is an excellent book written by an outstanding teacher. I have experienced the author's work at first hand. He enthuses, excites and captivates young and old alike.

The book tackles the thorny issues experienced by MFL teachers everywhere, i.e. how do students learn vocabulary? What is exciting is that he comes up with solutions which actually work, giving children 'more confidence and ... trust in the classroom, increasing their thirst for more knowledge.' I am not sure that you can ask much more than that!

At a time when behaviour in schools is a key area for Ofsted and the government, it is also worth noting that the use of Vocab Fun Learning Activities ensures that '*students engage in learning ... with the knock-on effect of creating better behaviour for learning, which in turn allows the teacher to impart knowledge more authoritatively.*' Brilliant!

In conclusion this book should be available in every school. It is inspirational, revolutionary, thought provoking and works ... just like the author.

Contents

Chapter 1

Introduction and Philosophy

My childhood summers meant staying in a *gîte* in Brittany. It wasn't just the *crêpes* I looked forward to, but entering another culture, visiting local *restaurants* and vast *hypermarchés* and experiencing the joy of conducting simple transactional exchanges using words in a 'foreign language'. Here were opportunities for bringing out my Collins French phrasebook and dictionary, not just for decoding the *panneaux de signalisation* and the *plats du jour*, but to sit quietly learning lists of vocabulary and phrases which I could then try out in real life scenarios. I could say things and make people react. I'd discovered this secret code! And the beginnings of a life-long passion.

In my first French lesson at secondary school my teacher gave me a present: a textbook to use in class and for homework. I was thrilled! Two weeks into Year 7, the teacher conducted a listening activity in class where we had to listen to the French football results from *Ligue 1* and write down the score: '*Paris Saint-Germain trois, Marseilles deux.*' It was just as well there were no 10-0 victories as we had only learned the numbers up to five. Such memories stick; I remember thinking, 'Wow, two of my favourite things in one class, football and languages!'

In Year 11, with exams looming, I had to revise for my German GCSE reading and listening papers. We had been told to 'learn your topic vocab!' With my Letts GCSE German Study Guide I locked myself away in my room and learned all of the vocabulary on all of the topic lists! When I heard *Holzhaus* I felt smug because this was a word I knew, perhaps picking up a mark that few other students would have got. I realised that language exams were basically about vocabulary.

As a trainee teacher, Newly Qualified Teacher (NQT) and Recently Qualified Teacher (RQT), I began to explore the transactional nature of teaching languages in general and of teaching vocabulary in particular. I had started my teaching career full of enthusiasm, armed with a textbook, a scheme of work and a stack of PowerPoint slides. My work in the classroom was driven by this familiar, well-trodden path; I needed to cover the course. It was a struggle keeping to the schedule, but I completed the textbook by April.

It was in my fourth year of teaching that I had to rethink my approach. I had hoped that this roadmap was serving my students well, but when their reading and listening exams came along many of the students found parts of the foundation reading paper difficult. One student said, 'I didn't know *gare routière*.' I said, 'Oh, it's only one mark. It's bus station, don't you remember? We did that in Year 10 when we did travel and holidays.' Well, had they remembered, they would have got the mark.

A colleague who had been teaching the top set told me that she never thought to teach the word *grève*, which the students needed to know in order to get a mark on the higher paper. I spent that summer holiday worrying about how I could ensure that every student knew words like *gare routière* and *grève*, which are part of everyday French life, not just words appearing on exam papers!

So, what to do? I was aware of the exam board's prescribed list of vocabulary, but I had never thought deeply about how to teach a word in Year 10 and be certain that the students would remember it for their exams in Year 11. Just because I could confidently say, 'I taught that word in Year 10, so if it comes up in an exam next year then great, I've done my job', it did not necessarily mean that the students would remember that word or recognise it when they saw or heard it.

I had been teaching vocabulary in the modern foreign languages classroom by writing the words on the Interactive Whiteboard, modelling the pronunciation, getting the students to repeat it, and checking their pronunciation. Towards the end of the lesson I measured their progress by asking the students to recall what they had learned. But even so, the students were not retaining the vocabulary. More was needed.

My personal way of learning vocabulary – which had been to simply stare at a list of words and repeat them to myself over and over again – was never going to inspire students. Nor did I think the best course of action would be to write to parents and recommend they buy their child a Collins French phrasebook and dictionary to read in their quiet moments. Instead, I asked myself:

- In my experience, how do students learn vocabulary?
- Can I identify which knowledge is more important for students to learn in order to improve their chances of success?
- Can I introduce activities in the classroom so that when I impart this knowledge the students remain engaged and motivated when practising it?
- Is there a more effective way of getting students to remember more content (vocabulary) over a longer period of time?

During my time as a trainee teacher on my PGCE and as an NQT, the best teachers I had seen had always struck me as 'entertaining content deliverers' (particularly with Year 7 classes). They imparted knowledge and practised the language in a variety of ways, all of which focused on learning through repetition. I had experienced some of this as a student in Year 7. My teacher used flashcards to present a picture, would say the word and get the class to repeat it. Once all the flashcards had been seen, we were presented with random cards and asked to identify them. Were we being exposed to as much language as possible during the lesson? Given that the teacher only showed one flashcard at a time, clearly not. Students could be shown far more words on a PowerPoint slide.

First, I had to let go of the old pattern. I had been creating PowerPoints with just one word or phrase on a slide. It dawned on me that I could expose students to far more vocabulary simply by putting more of it on the slide. The slide would still draw their attention, but now there was much more to see and learn. I would take advantage of the natural tendency to scan everything in sight. It was my own hunch, not based on any teaching and learning evidence.

This was a start. However, simply showing more words and relying on more repetition would not guarantee improving students' recall of the all-important vocabulary and grammar points. In the foreword to Lemov's *Practice Perfect*, Dan Heath stresses that it is not just repetition that improves performance but correct practice. You need the right kind of practice with the right mindset: it's not about being weak or bad. 'To practice is to declare, *I can be better*.'[1]

---

[1] D. Lemov et al., (2012) *Practice Perfect: 42 Rules for Getting Better at Getting Better*, San Francisco, Jossey-Bass. p. xiii.

Improving students' performance in the classroom involves conducting a combination of activities that keep students motivated and engaged over a period of time. They are repeating and practising the vocabulary with the teacher, and then deliberately practising retrieval. And when the students look back at what they were doing, they realise they were having fun! It's this strategy *over time* that has the greatest impact on their ability and attitude to learning a foreign language.

There were setbacks along the way. Students in the exam were still failing to recall vocabulary which they had covered the year before. I had taught this vocabulary, so why hadn't they known it? I remembered the second key question I had asked myself: can I identify which knowledge is more important for students to learn in order to improve their chances of success? Here was an opportunity to revise what I was doing. I analysed dozens of reading and listening papers, looking for recurring vocabulary which was essential for getting the marks on any reading or listening paper. For example, for my Spanish group the essentials were *los deportes acuáticos* (on the 2010 WJEC Reading paper) and *compartir*, which would greatly aid understanding to answering a question (on the 2010 AQA Higher Reading paper).

I compiled a list of words and the odd short phrase based on this frequency analysis; this became the Key Vocab List. You might say that some vocab is more important than other knowledge; although the exam board prescribes a set list of words, it is not ranked. Having prioritised this list of words and phrases, I put them on a PowerPoint, but I still needed to ensure that the students knew this vocabulary. I needed answers to my other questions: what kind of activities would engage and motivate the students? What was the most effective way of getting students to remember more content (vocabulary) for longer? Or to put it another way: how could I make it stick in a fun and engaging way so that I was almost tricking students into learning?

The words on the Key Vocab List came from different topics and in no particular order. Textbooks impose some arbitrary order based on topics, but there was no real reason for teaching vocabulary in that order just because that was how it appeared in a textbook or scheme of work. Learning had to be more flexible and allow for practice at getting key vocabulary into students' long-term memories. So whenever I taught a topic, I always included additional practice of key vocabulary unrelated to the topic.

With this philosophy in mind, I devised as many ways as I could think of to get the students to practise this key knowledge in class. I didn't think they would respond positively to vocab test after vocab test; however, being reasonably sporty, I realised that if the practice was competitive it would be more engaging. This, then, was the basis of the Vocab Fun Learning Activities (VFLAs) which focused on students practising the language in a fun way. All of the VFLAs involve the teacher standing at the front of the class showing a PowerPoint slide of key vocabulary on the board. To test retrieval, I constructed PowerPoint slides on which I could cover up the English meanings. For the competitive element, I divided the class in half with students on one side competing against the other.

Several VFLAs can be used in the same lesson to practise the knowledge and to test recall. Varied and spaced practice has proven successful in ensuring that students acquire core knowledge. In *Make It Stick*, the authors suggest the following:

> *To be most effective, retrieval must be repeated again and again, in spaced out sessions so that the recall, rather than becoming a mindless recitation, requires some cognitive effort. Repeated recall appears to help memory consolidate into a cohesive representation in the brain and to strengthen and multiply the neural routes by which the knowledge can later be retrieved.*[2]

I had been employing this practice-retrieval effect using the VFLAs with groups of students from Year 10 onwards (though when I started I wasn't aware of the theory behind it). The term 'retrieval' is now frequently used instead of 'test', not only because of the negative associations of that word, but because it more accurately describes what happens during recall.[3]

After some VFLAs using key vocabulary items, I would test retrieval by covering up the English meaning on the PowerPoint slide. The logic was that in order to do well on a reading and listening paper students do not necessarily need to be able to spell the Target Language word because the source material on these papers is always in the Target Language. Therefore, I was practising recognition-retrieval. Having covered up the English meaning I would then give the students some time in pairs or individually to write down the English meaning or I would conduct a different type of quiz to practise retrieval.

The VFLAs create competition between individual students, or teams, or each half of the class. Something as simple as telling the students that the pair who could write the greatest correct number of words from the slide would receive one of the language trophies (which I would give out, and at the end of the lesson take back in again) can act as a powerful motivator.

These class activities are not frivolous games. For me, the idea of a language *game* implies superficiality. In the past the well-known language game Splat (see FLA #23) always worked well *as a game*. However, did it allow all of the students to practise as much vocabulary as possible? Were all of the students involved all of the time? What were the other students doing while the splatters were doing their splatting? Was there an objective behind the practice that the students were aware of or was it just a way to wind down at the end of the lesson?

---

[2] P. C. Brown et al., (2014) *Make It Stick: The Science of Successful Learning*, Cambridge, MA, Harvard University Press. pp. 28–29.

[3] B. Carey, (2014) *How We Learn: The Surprising Truth about When, Where and Why it Happens*, London, Macmillan. p. 93.

Just showing a list of what would be, in the students' eyes, a list of arbitrary words would not be motivating. However, explaining how what they are doing in class is directed towards achieving exam success can be very powerful. This is why I talk about *selling* the idea, which means linking the activity with the long-term objective and encouraging the students to adopt a positive attitude towards learning.

To maximise learning, the students need to practise this key vocabulary at some time during every lesson or at least every other lesson. This provides *spaced practice*. By running VFLAs with the Year 10 class for the practice and retrieval of key vocabulary in every lesson, their exam results showed phenomenal improvements. This vindicated what I was doing in the eyes of the students. They could see the purpose of it and that it was working. This gave them more confidence and built trust in the classroom, increasing their thirst for more knowledge. The attitudes to learning changed and a climate of competition developed: a team of students and the teacher were now competing against the exam.

After the reading and listening exams, the students came to tell me just how easy they had found both exams. They rattled off words they recalled as answers to questions and said these were the easiest exams they had taken so far – a stark contrast to my first GCSE group. Come results day in August the Spanish results were incredible: the students had achieved 100% A*–C and 81% A*–A. The local media became interested with The Sentinel and Crewe Chronicle referring to them.[4] With the reading and listening results an overwhelming majority of students had exceeded their target grades.

I had proven to myself that with learning, engagement and progress I could help to achieve excellent outcomes for students. Furthermore, this approach led to fifteen students choosing to study Spanish beyond GCSE at AS level. Clearly these students did not perceive languages as too difficult.

The following year I adopted the VFLA practice with my Year 9 group but met some resistance when I suggested to a colleague that they could adopt part of this strategy in their own teaching. This belief that 'my students don't learn like that' is revealed as a fallacy when you examine what actually works for transferring as much knowledge as possible from a student's short-term memory to their long-term memory by revisiting it and practising it at spaced intervals. The way to convince colleagues is through results and students' performance – you must lead by example. But part of that example is demonstrating continuous improvement; there is still a long way to go. As language teachers, one of the ultimate goals is to create an environment where students are speaking the language independently. But this independence can only come once the students have a core body of knowledge with which to work.

---

4 See http://www.stokesentinel.co.uk/marks-students-lead-way-making-grade-host/story-13230386-detail/story.html and http://www.crewechronicle.co.uk/news/local-news/alsager-school-gcse-results-5607224.

The role of the teacher

The teacher's role is to inspire, engage, support and promote students' learning. Teachers also act as a role model for the students: just as the students practise vocabulary and other language features, the teacher is likewise practising teaching. Teaching is an art that has to be learned. The more you practise, the better you become, or as Parker Palmer puts it: 'Technique is what teachers use until the real teacher arrives.'[5]

Both teacher and students need to know that they are engaged in purposeful activity which will lead towards mastery. It's not about the teacher showing off their own knowledge but rather ensuring that the students are given enough opportunities to acquire their own body of knowledge.

Students must first acquire sufficient language knowledge and reach a basic level of automaticity with it. Year 7 students are initially dependent upon their teacher imparting all of the basic language knowledge that they need. You could think of the class as a *learning organism*, which collectively takes in the new information, and in which the individuals learn from each other, and from each other's mistakes. The more they hear, see and practise, the more likely they will achieve the broader goal of automaticity with the language.

The Ofsted framework grade descriptor for outstanding quality of teaching includes the following: 'Teachers and other adults authoritatively impart knowledge to ensure that pupils are engaged in learning, and generate high levels of commitment to learning across the school.'[6]

My experience of using the VFLAs is that students engage in learning and this has the knock-on effect of creating better behaviour for learning, which in turn allows the teacher to impart knowledge more authoritatively.

In my NQT year, there was an aversion to teacher-led lessons and teacher instruction. One observer commented that my lesson was 'very heavy on teacher talk', and that I needed to 'find ways of encouraging students to learn more independently'. I'm not sure how this Year 7 group could have worked independently, as this was a new topic and the class had not encountered any of the words before. Recent work by John Hattie, who has carried out a vast meta-analysis evaluating the success rates of different teaching approaches, has shown that direct instruction is one of the most powerful teaching factors. What this means in practice is that students are taught the knowledge first. They see the words in the Target Language, and the teacher models the pronunciation. Then they are free to practise this independently.

---

[5] J. Parker Palmer, (2007) *The Courage to Teach: Exploring the Inner Landscape of a Teacher's Life*, San Francisco, Jossey-Bass. p. 5.

[6] Ofsted, (2015) *School Inspection Handbook*. Ref: 120101. Available at: https://www.gov.uk/government/publications/school-inspection-handbook.

The VFLAs present the language content first; the students then practise this in an engaging way. Consistent engagement with the lessons is a huge factor in students opting whether to continue with further study of a language.

Fun Learning Activities

The FLAs are about sentence structure and ways to practise paragraph-building, and thus have a different function from the VFLAs, which focus on making vocabulary and short phrases stick and on moving as much language into students' long-term memories as possible.

The Fun Learning Activities (FLAs) came next. Most of the FLAs have the students working in groups, practising the language independently from the teacher. To a greater or lesser extent all of the FLAs rely on the students having already acquired the relevant background knowledge, such as basic sound-spelling links and the International Phonetic Alphabet in Pronuncistation Funology (FLA #34). Fast-Forwarded Learning (FLA #26) has the teacher record a clip of themselves teaching a grammatical point not yet covered with the class. During the showing of the clip the students are asked to note down how they think they could manipulate the grammar point themselves. However, in order that the students may complete the activity, this clip must refer to knowledge they have already acquired. That is why in the very first lesson with a Year 7 group it would be difficult to conduct a FLA without having first imparted and practised some vocabulary and grammatical knowledge using the VFLAs.

The aim, therefore, is first to impart the vocabulary knowledge that the students need and then to have the students demonstrate that they can use and adapt this knowledge in other contexts. The key message is that students' learning 'requires the guidance of teachers, the diligence of repeated practice and sustained effort in order to be achieved'.[7]

During a recent Ofsted inspection the Lead Inspector observed my lesson with a Year 7 Spanish group and included the following passage in the school's Ofsted report:

> *In the very best lessons, teachers use creative approaches to teaching which help students enjoy their learning and make considerable progress. For example, in two Year 7 Spanish lessons where the teaching was outstanding, teachers used imaginative and fast-paced activities to help students become confident in the new phrases. As a result, students proudly showed how fluent they had become in talking about likes and dislikes, showing excellent attitudes to learning.*[8]

---

[7] Robert Peal, (2014) *Progressively Worse: The Burden of Bad Ideas in British Schools*, London, Civitas. p. 194.

[8] Ofsted, (2013) *Inspection Report: Heart of England School*, 13–14 November. p. 5. See http://www.ofsted.gov.uk/inspection-reports/find-inspection-report/provider/ELS/136909.

In that lesson I used several VFLAs to practise knowledge of school subjects and opinion phrases.

Then the students went To The Walls (FLA #14) to build their own sentences on the Magic Whiteboards around the room (see Chapter 2). This is a technique I frequently use in order to get students to prove to me, other students, and most importantly to themselves that they are able to write well-formed sentences. Once I have checked what has been written, the students sign their names under their work as evidence that they can do this.

With changes afoot, where lessons will no longer be graded by Ofsted, it would seem that rather than just 'turning on the Ofsted lesson' and getting a one-off snapshot grading, you need to be able to explain and justify what you do in the classroom to help students progress in the long term. After all, this gives a fairer reflection of the quality of teaching and learning over time.

Reflection

One of the greatest effects on student learning, according to Hattie, comes when teachers reflect on and learn from their own teaching. I feel that the following points define outstanding teachers.

Outstanding teachers:

- Ensure that students engage fully with what is being taught;
- Develop strategies for teaching new content;
- Impart new knowledge, and then monitor students' learning by frequently testing retrieval of this new knowledge;
- Put themselves in the students' position to understand better how they are learning.[9]

The journey and reflection on my own practice has involved all of these bullet points. What I find so exciting is that these characteristics, not only are officially referred to in Hattie's research but, could apply to any teacher in any subject who is flexible in wanting to learn and adapt their own practice to improve outcomes for students. This book's activities and philosophy is my way of encouraging other teachers to do this.

In addition, teachers should be objective in their grading, and not use it to reward or punish students, and they should encourage students to think creatively, rather than using worksheets which can reduce engagement and limit thought.[10]

---

[9] J. Hattie, (2012) *Visible Learning For Teachers: Maximizing Impact on Learning*, Abingdon, Routledge. p. 23.

[10] Hattie, (2012) p. 36.

I hope that the idea of the VFLAs and FLAs supported by the attitudes to teaching described here with reference to Hattie will lead to success for both students and teachers in their own journey of language-learning and teaching.

Chapter 2

Magic Whiteboards and Mini-Whiteboards

Willkommen in Berlin — BRANDENBURG GATE

The traditional layout in most classrooms (depending on the subject) is to have a whiteboard (one you can write on with a marker pen) or an Interactive Whiteboard (IAW), or both, at the front of the room. This was not the case for my first classroom as an NQT. There was an IAW at the front of the class and a whiteboard on the right-hand side of the room, so if I wanted to write anything on the whiteboard I had to march over to one side of the room to write on it with a marker pen and then march back to the front to work my limited IAW magic.

I had a working knowledge of how to use the IAW but I found that when issues occurred, such as the pen-nib not connecting with the board or the board having to be recalibrated, this led to a loss of lesson and learning time. There was little value for the students watching me clicking on the wrong things or trying to find a pen with a working nib. The only thing they were learning was perhaps that there is sometimes a more straightforward way to make the most of learning time than using new classroom technology just for the sake of using it.

Regardless of my technical proficiency at using the IAW (which was never going to eclipse the average Year 8 student's tech-savvy skills), if I couldn't give timely feedback to the students efficiently then my own ICT skills didn't matter. I needed a board on which I could rely, one board upon which I could instantly write bits of language that the students might need, and another board next to that on which there was an image or text *projected* that I was using as the language source.

One weekend I solved the problem of having easier access to a whiteboard by going out and buying one myself. This board was on wheels, and the next Monday morning I rolled it down the corridor past the head teacher's office and into the corner of my classroom right next to the IAW. However, once I'd put the whiteboard-on-wheels next to the IAW, there wasn't an awful lot of space at the front of my classroom; I'd literally trapped myself into a corner – a slave to teaching and learning! Eventually I had a fixed whiteboard fitted next to the IAW but kept the whiteboard-on-wheels in the corner. Occasionally I asked students to write up sentence examples on that wheelie-whiteboard as an extension task, and this corner became known as the 'extension-task corner'.

When students finished a long piece of written work I found that the wheelie-whiteboard in the corner worked a little like a visualiser (a piece of hardware that projects whatever you put under it) in that it revealed their perfections or imperfections which I and the rest of the class were then able to see and comment on. Whiteboards make progress (or lack thereof) *visible*, and enable both teacher and students to assess if others have 'got it' or not. They also allow instant corrective feedback: students write, you tell them which bits are right or wrong and why, and they correct it right there and then in front of you. As Lemov reminds us, giving speedy feedback leads to success.[1]

This encouraged me to use mini-whiteboards more often. I've always been a fan of the mini-whiteboard, and was fascinated to learn that Ross Morrison McGill has one stitched to his apron, another to the outside door of his classroom and one more to his planner.[2] I like the idea, as McGill puts it, that mini-whiteboards can 'help solve problems with students one-on-one, or in small groups around a table, without the need to stop a whole class from working'.[3]

A practical way of providing more flexible writing space came from a technological advance.

---

[1] Lemov, (2012) p. 117.

[2] Ross Morrison McGill, (2013) *100 Ideas for Secondary Teachers: Outstanding Lessons*, London, Bloomsbury Education. p. 4.

[3] McGill, (2013) p. 4.

The Magic Whiteboard™ was demonstrated in an episode of *Dragons' Den* in 2008.[4] This is a reusable and removable thin film plastic writing surface which you can easily stick to the wall. By sticking several Magic Whiteboards (MWBs) around my walls there would be enough writing space for several pairs of students to use. Another advantage of these whiteboards is that they can be stuck over doors, cupboards, windows and parts of displays, and easily cleaned or removed at the end of the lesson.

I'm not advocating using MWBs as a universal solution; they are just alternatives to the mini-whiteboards. Many of the FLAs can be adapted to be used on mini-whiteboards. (In this book, I'll refer to the Magic Whiteboard™ as MWB, and the mini-whiteboard as, well, mini-whiteboard.)

By sticking several pieces of MWB up around the classroom I was aiming to:

- Enable students to model longer written examples for the whole class to see.
- Create mini-classrooms within a classroom.
- Create a gallery of 'work in progress' and modelling to be displayed during lessons.
- Vary the more traditional approach of students with mini-whiteboards facing the teacher.

The aim was not to replace mini-whiteboards but to add flexibility in the classroom. At that time I was not aware of other teaching and learning organisations using MWBs as I was planning to do. However, I have since discovered that it has been adopted in all of the 140 BusyBees and LeapFrog nurseries.

Andrew Old's educational blog (Scenes From The Battleground) refers to the use of mini-whiteboards in a school he worked in. To a post asking what the issue with mini-whiteboards is his response was that they sometimes seem to be forced on teachers when it simply isn't worth it. Old is not attacking mini-whiteboards per se. He says, 'They can be useful but they should not be obligatory.' He also illustrates negative points about the use of mini-whiteboards:

I observed a top set RE lesson where students were instructed to write 'arguments for and against the existence of God' on mini-whiteboards. These were high achieving (and highly coached) kids. A lot of them were writing mini-essays that were virtually unreadable.

I have seen PGCE students struggle to manage classes with mini-whiteboards and also spend hours trying to sort, clean and find a full set to use. It is not something that all classes are receptive to, yet they were convinced that they were required to try it.[5]

---

4 See http://www.magicwhiteboard.co.uk/.

5 Andrew Old, (2010) 'The Outstanding School', *Scenes From The Battleground* (blog). See https://teachingbattleground.wordpress.com/2010/11/22/the-outstanding-school/.

The first point Old makes was one of the reasons why I thought it would be better to use MWBs rather than mini-whiteboards: they simply have a lot more space for students to write on. Mini-whiteboards are roughly A4 size, and MWBs are 60cm by 80cm; the same size as flip chart paper.

A number of FLAs refer to using MWBs. Having them up around the classroom means that students have instant access to writing words, sentences or short paragraphs and the teacher can use what has been written as a way of assessment for learning. They are also ideal for a teacher with no classroom base. Using MWBs also removes from the teacher the impracticality of frequently handing out mini-whiteboards and taking them in again, should they rely solely on mini-whiteboards.

However, bear in mind that there are one or two advantages that mini-whiteboards have over the MWB. For example, every student has their own mini-whiteboard. You would need a lot of space around the classroom to provide every student in a class of thirty with a MWB to write on. Even one between two might be pushing it a bit.

You might not want to leave MWBs up throughout the year, but if they are left up on the wall they immediately remind the students of what they learned in a previous lesson. If they have been wiped clean, students can practise retrieval so, provide a set of marker pens on a desk at the front and as they come in, tell them to get a pen and spend the next five minutes writing all that they can remember about a previous topic on a MWB.

Mini-classrooms

Arranging MWBs around the classroom creates separate mini-classroom spaces where students can work in small groups. Practically you would need to put at least ten MWBs around the room. The students will then be able to practise their language on the boards and the teacher will be able to observe and assess what has been learned. In this way, the MWBs can be seen as learning boards or progress boards.

They can function, as my wheelie-whiteboard did, as extension boards where students write up what they've written in their books. Stick several MWBs around the room and then during the lesson, when a student tells you that they've finished some written work in their book, instead of going over to check it and feed back to the student individually, you ask them to write up what they have put in their books on a MWB so that you and the class can comment on it. Or you might first give the student some feedback on what they've written so that they correct it *and then* go and write it up; you are then using that student's answer as a model of good practice. With several MWBs around the room many more students can work this way than on a mini-whiteboard. Using MWBs not only makes progress more visible, it means students are able to look across the class at other boards, see what other students are doing, and be inspired by it.

Using the whiteboards in practice

When I developed VFLAs like Bob-Up Classic (VFLA #1) and Señor Hunton Dice (VFLA #15) I started the activities in my traditional place at the front of the room, imparting vocabulary knowledge and modelling the correct pronunciation before beginning the VFLAs. However, thinking more deeply about the FLAs, I realised that what I was doing at the front of the class could easily be replicated by students in small groups at MWBs around the room.

To test this, I chose a class who were particularly motivated to try new activities and explained what I was trying to do: this would be Group Bob-Up (VFLA #11) with groups of three students placed at every MWB. Each group assigned one student to be the teacher-student leading Bob-Up. The teacher-student would call out the Target Language or the English for any of the words projected on a PowerPoint slide on the board at the front of the class. The other two students in each group would be sitting facing the projected list. The first to identify the Target Language word for the English word the teacher-student called out would bob up and say both the English and Target Language and win a point.

This meant that I could carry out most of the VFLAs and create more FLAs using this set-up. In other words, I was maximising opportunities for the students to practise their language knowledge in their own 'classroom within a classroom'.

I also use the MWBs to demonstrate progress during lessons. Whenever I want students to show anyone just how much they have learned in a lesson, I tell them to get a board pen and write the vocabulary, short phrases, verb conjugation, exam paper pitfalls and so on, on any one of the MWBs on the classroom walls – and get the students to sign their names under what they have written.

Chapter 3

Introduction to the Vocab Fun Learning Activities (VFLAs)

The teacher is defined by the vocabulary teaching strategies he or she uses.

Višnja Pavičić Takač[1]

It's not only having vocabulary strategies but *how* they are used by the teacher that matters.

In Chapter 1, I insisted that VFLAs are not games. I correct the students when they refer to them as games and half-jokingly reinforce that by saying, 'They're not games, they're Fun *Learning* Activities.' I even get them to repeat that back in order to emphasise positive

---

1 Višnja Pavičić Takač, (2008) *Vocabulary Learning Strategies and Foreign Language Acquisition*, Clevedon, Multilingual Matters. p. 106.

learning behaviour. Fun without the learning implies a missing objective and a lack of strategy supporting their use. To reiterate, VFLAs are used for practising vocabulary knowledge with the students before the teacher tests retrieval.

In this section and throughout the descriptions of the VFLAs I use the terms 'testing recall', 'testing retrieval', 'practising retrieval' and 'retrieval-practice' interchangeably. They all describe the process of testing the students' knowledge of the vocabulary once they have practised the language knowledge and have been encouraged to think about meaning.

The nature of VFLAs ensures that students repeat the Target Language words aloud, rather than silently. Research has shown that repeating words aloud increases retention rates far more effectively than silent repetition. This makes for a noisy, exciting, competitive, engaged and ultimately knowledge-rich classroom, and results in confident, interested, motivated, knowledge-rich and, ultimately, skilled students.

The VFLAs are not intended to be used in isolation, with, for example, just one VFLA at the end of the lesson. Instead, a good strategy is for the teacher to select four, five, or even six different VFLAs to get students to practise vocabulary and short phrases spaced over a number of lessons throughout the half-term, term, year or course. A term or academic year's worth of teaching and learning would involve a range of VFLAs. Variety is good. Through the process of experimentation, the teacher learns to judge which VFLAs are best suited to a particular class and for the next topic.

VFLAs are rapid fire, so keep up the pace. The more words called out, the greater the practice. I have used six or seven VFLAs to practise one slide of key vocabulary in a twenty-minute spell with a class before practising retrieval. In *Teach Like a Champion*, Doug Lemov comments, 'the art is in the discretionary application of the techniques … There is a right and wrong time and place for every tool, and it will always fall to the unique style and vision of great teachers to apply them.'[2]

Changing a VFLA helps refocus students' attention. A few minutes using one VFLA with a class followed by a quick, slick change to another VFLA grabs students' attention and keeps them engaged. Willingham, in *Why Don't Students Like School?*, recommends change as it promotes attention, and thus enhances students' engagement and therefore their learning.[3] He also says that when changing topics or starting a new activity the students' attention needs to come back to the teacher, thus providing the teacher with a further opportunity to engage the students.[4]

---

[2] Doug Lemov, (2010) *Teach Like a Champion: 49 Techniques That Put Students on the Path to College,* San Francisco, Jossey-Bass. p. 13.

[3] D. T. Willingham, (2009) *Why Don't Students Like School?*, San Francisco, Jossey-Bass. p. 165.

[4] Willingham, (2009) p. 22.

Automaticity

Practising vocabulary knowledge with the VFLAs aims to move students further towards automaticity with the key vocabulary that frequently occurs on the reading and listening sections of the exam. Ron Martinez, in *Debates in Modern Languages Education*, discusses the concept of having a certain threshold vocabulary which allows students to achieve a level of performance appropriate to their 'learning needs'.[5] Students' learning needs in the context of the GCSE exams are essentially based on the breadth of knowledge of key vocabulary (how many words they know) with some degree of depth (how the words are used in the culture, and their variety of forms and connections). Whatever topic the students are learning, they need to develop a 'mental lexicon', and these VFLAs work well as a means of doing this. A third factor Martinez discusses is that of fluency: '… another important dimension of the mental lexicon is how readily one is able to recall and use a word, and the ease with which it is used'.[6] This is also referred to as 'automaticity', and this is the term I shall be using here.

At GCSE level, though, is it realistic to expect that in the two (or three) years that you have with a class for two lessons a week that all the students' mental lexicons have the breadth, depth and fluency of all of the course vocabulary in their second language (L2)? To what degree has their language knowledge been enhanced so that they are fully confident in all three areas of all of the course vocabulary?

One thing I would want for my students at GCSE, particularly on the reading paper, is for them to have a good *breadth* of knowledge of key vocabulary and common expressions as they go into the exam. I also want them to have *depth* in their vocabulary knowledge and for them to demonstrate the level of automaticity that I consider essential. The degree to which this can be achieved depends on the length of time I spend with a class over the course and the amount of exposure to and practice with the Target Language I can provide.

Martinez also refers to a study carried out by Waring and Takaki (2003) on incidental exposure to new words.[7] Although there is little evidence that this is an efficient means of learning vocabulary, it does help build depth. The more that students are exposed to words in other contexts, the more likely they are to learn something of the variety and subtleties of meaning the words have in combination with others.

---

[5] R. Martinez in P. Driscoll, E. Macaro, and A. Swarbrick, (Eds) (2014) *Debates in Modern Languages Education*, Abingdon, Routledge. p. 121.

[6] Martinez in Driscoll et al., (2014) p. 123.

[7] Martinez in Driscoll et al., (2014) pp. 132–133.

It's also important to remember that learning a MFL is more than just acquiring new words; students need to continually revisit words they know (or think they know). This is where the spaced practice is important: teaching the language knowledge, revisiting the knowledge and practising it again in a variety of ways before testing retrieval. Practising vocabulary with the VFLAs and testing retrieval needs to be spaced out throughout a term, academic year or GCSE course. I would not expect all students in the class to retain every word or phrase practised using VFLAs at the end of one week.

It is also important, in between practice with the VFLAs and before testing retrieval, to draw students' attention in some way to the *meaning* of what has just been practised. One way of doing this is to discuss with the students their favourite sounding words. (Another is to have students assembling sentences into meaningful paragraphs, such as in several FLAs.)

The idea of spaced practice and retrieval practice, as described in *Make It Stick*, is supported by Pimsleur's Memory Schedule, which emphasises the importance of asking students or *testing* students on their recall.[8]

Paul Pimsleur was a talented scholar who worked in the field of applied linguistics and developed the Pimsleur Language Learning System based on spaced repetition. An interesting and particularly relevant quote from the *Modern Language Journal*, to which Pimsleur contributed, sums up the strategy of the VFLAs very well:

> *The teacher should recall the item very frequently right after it is first presented, though interspersed with other activities which take the student's mind off it between recalls.*[9]

Let's call the VFLAs these 'other activities'. The recalls can be direct teacher questioning of students about what a word means or quizzing the whole class on their recall of vocabulary by projecting a list of words on the board, covering up the English meaning and telling the students to write as many meanings as possible down in x minutes.

The teacher could use VFLAs on a different slide to take students' minds off the first slide, and after a while revisit that slide and test recall of the original list. The combination of using VFLAs to practise key vocabulary with a class, testing students' recall and then reminding them of the correct answer returns the students' knowledge of the word to 100%.

Clearly, the longer that the teacher leaves it after VFLA practice before testing students' recall, the lower the chances that the student will recall the word correctly. This is well illustrated by Pimsleur's graph.[10]

---

8 Brown et al., (2014) pp. 3–4.

9 P. Pimsleur, (1967) 'A Memory Schedule', *Modern Language Journal* (51: 75). p. 75.

10 See Graph 3, Pimsleur, (1967) p. 75.

Another key piece here is to test the students' recall once practised. With the Spanish group referred to in Chapter 1, I spaced out the recall of key exam vocabulary throughout the lessons during the final year. Pimsleur refers to this as 'graduated interval recall'.

I don't mind admitting that at the time I wasn't aware of the theory behind this practice. I adopted this methodology because I found that it had a significant impact on students' performance in past reading and listening papers, and that the students became greatly animated in lessons.

Practising vocabulary using VFLAs is engaging. But testing retrieval? Well, not every single action in a classroom has to be engaging. I would do my best in testing individual students' recall arbitrarily by asking them questions of the kind Pimsleur refers to, such as, 'Do you remember how to excuse yourself in Greek?'[11] In my NQT year I developed a rule that at the end of every lesson I would say to the students, 'Quickest side to tell me what *x* means', 'Quickest side to tell me any four words learned today' or, 'Quickest side to tell me any two past tense and two future tense phrases learned today.' Essentially, I was conducting a plenary in which I was testing students' recall. In this way, you are testing their progress of learning vocabulary. Indeed, Jackie Beere refers to needing to 'take a moment for a mini-plenary at any time in the session to gather evidence about the learning progress.'[12]

To sum up: practise what you want students to learn, show what the students have learned and demonstrate their progress through testing their recall.

Motivation and challenge

Although motivating and engaging students to practise learning vocabulary with you in class with a repertoire of VFLAs is all well and good, motivating students while testing their recall is just as important.

In *Motivating Students to Learn*, Jere Brophy entitled one of the sections of his book 'Competition: A powerful but problematic extrinsic incentive'.[13] What matters is how the teacher 'sells' the phase of practising vocabulary retrieval to the students. Andy Griffith and Mark Burns point out that there is a cognitive switch made from extrinsic motivation to intrinsic motivation which involves changing the students' mindsets from *having* to recall

---

[11] Pimsleur, (1967) p. 74.

[12] J. Beere, (2012) *The Perfect Ofsted Lesson*, Carmarthen, Independent Thinking Press. p. 37.

[13] J. Brophy, (2004) *Motivating Students to Learn*, Abingdon, Routledge. p. 171.

this vocabulary (the extrinsic motivation) to *wanting* to recall this vocabulary (the intrinsic motivation).[14]

I have always found challenge to be a successful motivator that gets students engaged when practising retrieval. Challenge is one of the Eight Triggers mentioned by Griffith and Burns as being a great motivating technique; accepting challenge is an effective way of obtaining results.[15]

Here is one way to create challenge. Project a slide of key vocabulary on the board, have the students practise the vocabulary with VFLAs, and then project a slide with the English translations covered up as in Figure 1, which introduces the retrieval stage.

Note that some of the numbered lines opposite have lots more key vocabulary than others. When conducting the VFLAs, the students are expected to say the whole numbered line of vocabulary and phrases and not just the first word on the line. So, for line 15, a student would say all of the French and the English for these weather terms. Having practised the vocabulary meanings, I then test students' retrieval by covering up the English as in Figure 1.

Personal challenges – such as students beating their personal best on the number of words that they can recall – work well. Therefore, I say to the students that they have five minutes to write as many words as possible that they can recall from the projected slide.

Another thing that works well in my own lessons is to award trophies and medals to the students who achieve the top five scores of recalled vocabulary. However, I can understand Brophy's concerns with giving extrinsic rewards. Brophy does, however, state that, 'winners are congratulated but losers are not criticized or ridiculed; the accomplishments of the class as a whole … are acknowledged'.[16] A way to depersonalise the retrieval-practice stage is to have the students competing as pairs or as groups of three and to write as many words down as possible that they can recall. Even if one student in the group cannot recall a word and another student can, then the student who could not recall the word initially is reminded of the meaning, putting their knowledge of the word back up to the 100% that Pimsleur refers to. They are reminded of the meaning by their peers and as they are part of a team the burden of not knowing the word is softened by a team member knowing it.

The competitive nature of the VFLAs and practising retrieval of vocabulary have a great deal to do with the *rapport* between the teacher and the class. Rapport is another of the Eight Triggers

---

[14] A. Griffith and M. Burns, (2012) *Outstanding Teaching: Engaging Learners*, Carmarthen, Crown House Publishing. p. 61.

[15] Griffith and Burns, (2012) p. 61.

[16] Brophy, (2004) p. 172.

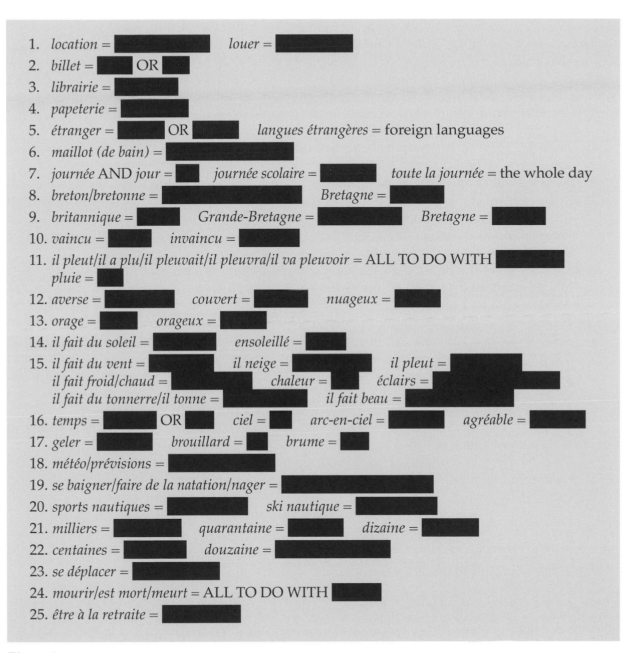

1. *location* = ███████   *louer* = ███████
2. *billet* = ████ OR ███
3. *librairie* = ██████
4. *papeterie* = █████████
5. *étranger* = ██████ OR ███████   *langues étrangères* = foreign languages
6. *maillot (de bain)* = █████████████
7. *journée AND jour* = ████   *journée scolaire* = ████████   *toute la journée* = the whole day
8. *breton/bretonne* = █████████████   *Bretagne* = ██████████
9. *britannique* = ██████   *Grande-Bretagne* = ████████   *Bretagne* = ████████
10. *vaincu* = ██████   *invaincu* = ████████
11. *il pleut/il a plu/il pleuvait/il pleuvra/il va pleuvoir* = ALL TO DO WITH ███████████
    pluie = ████
12. *averse* = ██████████   *couvert* = █████████   *nuageux* = ██████
13. *orage* = ██████   *orageux* = ███████
14. *il fait du soleil* = █████████   *ensoleillé* = ██████
15. *il fait du vent* = █████████   *il neige* = █████████   *il pleut* = ███████████
    il fait froid/chaud = █████████   *chaleur* = ██████   *éclairs* = █████████████
    il fait du tonnerre/il tonne = █████████████   *il fait beau* = ███████████
16. *temps* = ███████ OR █████   *ciel* = ████   *arc-en-ciel* = ████████   *agréable* = ██████████
17. *geler* = ███████   *brouillard* = ████   *brume* = ██████
18. *météo/prévisions* = █████████████
19. *se baigner/faire de la natation/nager* = █████████████████████
20. *sports nautiques* = █████████████   *ski nautique* = █████████████
21. *milliers* = █████████   *quarantaine* = ████████   *dizaine* = █████████
22. *centaines* = █████████   *douzaine* = ███████████
23. *se déplacer* = █████████
24. *mourir/est mort/meurt* = ALL TO DO WITH █████████
25. *être à la retraite* = █████████

Figure 1

and is an important factor in motivating students to want to work with and for the teacher.[17] This means that one of the aims of the lesson is to get the students wanting to practise retrieval *because they want to build a strong relationship with the teacher and show their respect.*

Making students aware of their own progress and celebrating this with all students is an incredibly powerful tool. In its most basic terms it could go something like this:

1. Project a slide of key vocabulary with the English meaning covered up like the slide shown in Figure 1.
2. At the start of the lesson ask students to read the Target Language vocabulary and phrases from the top to the bottom of the list and to write down the total number that they are 100% certain they know the English meaning of.
3. Project the same slide of key vocabulary but with the English meanings shown (remove the text boxes).
4. Practise several VFLAs with the class using this slide of key vocabulary and use some of the suggested strategies for getting students to think about the meaning of the vocabulary just practised.
5. Project the slide of key vocabulary with the English meanings covered up again.
6. Ask students to re-read the Target Language vocabulary and phrases from the top to the bottom of the list and to tally the total number of Target Language vocabulary and phrases that they are now 100% certain they know the English meaning of and write down the total.
7. Ask if the number of vocabulary and phrases they now know has increased.
8. Discuss, accentuate and celebrate the positive impact on their vocabulary learning in such a short space of time.
9. Then show the students a past reading paper or a past listening paper transcript containing some of the key vocabulary you have just shown and accentuate the 'You can do this' factor.

If you were to ask, 'What happens if the students' knowledge of vocabulary and phrases has not increased?' then I would say that you need to ensure that enough time has been dedicated to practising the vocabulary with VFLAs before practising retrieval.

I have used a variety of VFLAs to practise vocabulary knowledge and then projected a slide with that same vocabulary knowledge covered up, drilling the whole class by standing at the front and calling out the Target Language vocabulary from the first number down to the last, pausing a second to let the whole class call out the meaning. This is rapid fire stuff, certainly not vapid fire stuff! If you think about this in terms of Pimsleur's methodology, then the knowledge of those students who don't know the meaning of the covered-up word is brought back up to 100% by those in the class who *do* call out the correct meaning.

---

[17] Griffith and Burns, (2012) p. 60.

The names of each VFLA and FLA are designed to act as a common language between teacher and student and help to build rapport. Once a class is familiar with how the VFLA works, they will respond to the teacher simply saying the name of the VFLA. Immediately, the class is prepared for the next activity. Always use the name of the VFLA as a way of reducing what Doug Lemov in *Practice Perfect* calls the 'transaction cost'.[18] This is the amount of resources it takes to execute an exchange. It is more time-efficient for the teacher to tell the class that it's now time for Bob-Up Classic or Vlotto than explain how it works again. Having a specific name for the VFLAs also helps to build rapport and to create a supportive, shared identity between class teacher and students. As Lemov puts it, 'A shared vocabulary wins games, inspires teachers, steals bases, and brings people together.'[19]

How much vocabulary on one slide?

Traditionally, vocabulary has been introduced a word or phrase at a time. However, this is not the most effective way of doing things. I used to spend hours preparing PowerPoints comprising ten or so slides, each with a Target Language question at the top of the slide and a Target Language sentence at the bottom and a nice picture inserted in between the two sentences. I would run through the PowerPoint and get individual students to speak the phrases out loud on each slide. Then I realised that it would be more efficient to maximise the number of times learners faced vocabulary items.

VFLAs are intended to be used with the teacher showing students a lot of vocabulary. The strategy of projecting as much key vocabulary as possible on the board to a class is similar to that of 'Input Flooding' where students must notice what they learn.[20] Packing the vocabulary onto a PowerPoint slide and projecting it to the class means that 'learners are bombarded by an artificially increased number of the target form'.[21]

Any concerns over students' working memory being overloaded are alleviated as the projected PowerPoint slide of Target Language words and phrases *with the English next to each* acts as a

---

[18] Lemov, (2012) p. 184.

[19] Lemov, (2012) p. 185.

[20] Touran Ahour, Nima Pajoman and Nasrin Hadidi Tamjid, (2013) 'The Effect of Vocabulary Flooding Technique on Iranian EFL Elementary Learners' Vocabulary Learning', *International Journal of Applied Linguistics & English Literature*, Vol. 2 No. 6; November. pp. 185–193. See http://www.academia.edu/5329417/The-effect-of-vocabulary-flooding-on-Iranian-EFL-elementarylearners-vocabulary-learning.

[21] Samuel Francis, (2003) 'Input Flooding and the Acquisition of the Spanish Verbs Ser and Estar for Beginning-Level Adult Learners', PhD thesis, Purdue University, Lafayette, IN. See http://docs.lib.purdue.edu/dissertations/AAI3113799/.

memory aid supporting students' working memory. It is only when you cover up the meanings that you are testing students' recall.

Spacing out practice of the VFLAs and giving students more frequent exposure to vocabulary is similar to that of the vocabulary flooding technique referred to in a study by Touran Ahour and his colleagues. In the study the researchers write, 'vocabulary flooding in this study is defined as increasing the number of times that learners face vocabulary items'.[22] However, students' success comes not just from facing vocabulary items but in actively engaging with them.

VFLAs and FLAs in the classroom

The VFLAs and FLAs are intended to be used as part of *varied practice* and *spaced practice* in the classroom. They are for practising language knowledge, moving knowledge to students' long-term memories, getting students excited about learning languages and ultimately getting students to make outstanding progress. You could say that it's about Team MFL gathering high numbers of students opting for languages at GCSE and A level.

Throughout the descriptions of the VFLAs and the FLAs I frequently refer to resources that are projected onto the board at the front of the class. Given a conventional classroom seating plan, with students sitting at desks facing the board, it is easy to divide the class to create two sides or teams of students.

In the VFLA descriptions and instructions the generic term 'board' refers to the board at the front of the classroom, whether the traditional type of whiteboard, or an Interactive Whiteboard (IAW). I assume your classroom will have some kind of projector and some form of screen onto which you can display or project PowerPoint slides, again, either an IAW or whiteboard. Both are fine. The important thing about the slides is that they present the students with a lot of vocabulary at once. It doesn't even have to be PowerPoint; just as long as there is a list of, say, twenty-five to thirty words shown. When I do refer to whiteboards, this is a whiteboard on which you can write using a marker pen (so not the IAW).

It is not essential to number the vocabulary lists, but it will make life easier for you and the students most of the time you are using the VFLAs. ('Number the knowledge' is a phrase that I hope will catch on.) If you number the knowledge you want the students to practise, it gives you faster ways to identify that knowledge. For instance, by numbering a list of key

---

[22] Touran et al., (2013) p. 186.

vocabulary and conducting the Penalty Shoot-Out (VFLA #13) with a class, you make *how* the students choose the word more manageable. They can discuss which words they think their classmates (who cannot see the list on the board) will or will not get by discussing the *numbers* (even in the Target Language!) identifying each word or phrase. It avoids the sides 'giving the VFLA away'. (I wasn't going to say 'giving the *game* away', was I?)

For example, as in Figure 2 (on page 28), students might say, 'Don't do twelve, they'll know that' or 'Do nineteen, they'll never get that.'

Then again, when using Bob-Up Classic (VFLA #1), instead of your student captains giving out numbers to their classmates, they could use the Target Language words (and English meanings) instead. Pimsleur's view is that a student's knowledge is brought back up to 100% when they are reminded of the meaning of the word, so this might be a more effective way of squeezing some more knowledge practice in. By assigning a word to a student, the captain practises the language knowledge by telling the student the word, and both will be reminded of its meaning.

Any opportunity to involve repetition and remind students of the meaning of words is a good use of time. Although giving out numbers is quicker, what you gain in time you lose in terms of extra practice. It's a minor point but worth considering when constructing your vocabulary list.

Figure 2 has Target Language words and phrases which sometimes appear as a one-off word – #25. *vecinos* = neighbours, and others which take the whole line – #28. Students would be expected to say the *whole line* of Target Language and English meaning, regardless of whether there is just one word or a series of words and phrases. Tell them to 'Say what you see.'

Many VFLAs have students competing one side against the other. This works well with a traditional classroom layout. By dividing the class into two, they know which side they are on – that's what matters. As long as they are clear, you're ready to start practising language knowledge with the VFLAs.

If your room has a different layout then rather than spend time rearranging the seating, simply ask the students to form two teams making sure that this is based on an easily visible distinction.

There are times when having a set of tables in groups of five or six is a good idea. You could conduct VFLAs and award points according to the students who win the point for their group at each set of tables. Aim for flexibility. For example, when conducting a Relay (FLA #3) you want your students in small groups; when conducting Four Skills, Four Corners (FLA #2) you would want your students in a group. As Phil Beadle says, 'Having your tables in five groups

1. *apagar las luces/el ordenador* = to turn off the lights / the computer
2. *quedarse* AND *encontrarse con* = to meet   OR *quedarse* = to remain
3. *tras* = after
4. *instalaciones* = facilities   (*instalaciones deportivas* = sports facilities)
5. *limpio* = clean   *limpieza* = cleaning
6. *poco* = little   (*hay poca sombra* = there is little shade)
    poco + adjective = un- or in-   (*poco interesante* = uninteresting
    poco sano = unhealthy   *poco probable* = improbable)
7. *¡Qué pena!* = What a shame!
8. *los/las demás* = the rest / the others
9. *hacer turismo* = to do sight-seeing
10. *bañarse/nadar/hacer la natación* = to go swimming
11. *pescar/ir de pesca/hacer pesca* = to go fishing   *pescado* = fish
12. *molestar* AND *fastidiar* = to bother / annoy   (*me fastidia* = it annoys me)
    es molesto = it is annoying
13. *feria* = fair
14. *pantalla* = screen (computer / TV / cinema)
15. *alquilar* = to rent   *películas alquiladas* = rented films   *alquiler* = rent
16. *probar* = to try on (clothes) OR to try   (*probar drogas* = to try drugs)
17. *reembolso* = refund
18. *ambiente* = atmosphere   *medio ambiente* = environment
19. *comportarse* = to behave   *comportamiento* = behaviour
20. *hacer falta* = to be necessary
21. *estar en paro/parado* = to be unemployed   *desempleo* = unemployment
22. *los sin techo* = the homeless
23. *pelear* = to fight   *peleas* = fights
24. *inquietarse* AND *preocuparse* = to worry
25. *vecinos* = neighbours
26. *esperar* = to wait OR to hope
27. *volver* = to return   *la vuelta* = return
28. *descargar* AND *bajar* = to download   *descarga* = download
29. *billete* = ticket (train, etc.)   *entrada* = ticket (cinema, etc.)
    billete de ida = single   *billete de ida y vuelta* = return

Figure 2

of six is the optimum classroom layout, in that it allows you to mix up the activities'.[23] Let the learning activity and how the students work and learn best govern how you adapt the seating plan to get the best out of the students. What matters with the VFLAs is that all the students can see the lists of projected vocabulary and phrases.

The VFLAs, FLAs and technology

Some of the FLAs and VFLAs require the use of a digital video camera (such as the Flip video camera) or a digital Dictaphone; for example, in Fast-Forwarded Learning (FLA #26), the Scheme of Learning Trailer (FLA #27) and Digital Feedback (FLA #16). Use ICT to the best of your ability when running the FLAs and the VFLAs. If you need help in using ICT elements then I recommend Joe Dale's superb blog, where you will find many excellent ideas on incorporating ICT into MFL (I refer to this later in the Digital Feedback FLA #16).[24] Technology will inevitably change, and you will no doubt find better ways to run the VFLAs and FLAs.

Now let's have a look at these VFLAs.

---

[23] Phil Beadle, (2010) *How to Teach*, Carmarthen, Crown House Publishing. p. 7.

[24] See http://joedale.typepad.com/.

Chapter 4

The Vocab Fun Learning Activities (VFLAs)

Le pardon de sainte-Anne-d'Auray

The philosophy behind all of the VFLAs is that as many as possible of the class are involved and that the teacher uses whatever means to show as much language knowledge as possible to all the students during the VFLA. A sample list of key vocabulary is shown for each VFLA and they are available for download at www.crownhouse.co.uk/featured/fun-mfl. This could be a page from a textbook covering a specific topic, or a list of words the students have found challenging. Include some words and phrases which are essential but unrelated to the topic.

There are 18 VFLAs:

1 Bob-Up Classic (VFLA)

Bob-Up Classic is a prime example of practising language knowledge already imparted and testing retrieval. The idea of Bob-Up Classic came from observing a teacher who used the following method in her Spanish lesson. She had packs of ten cards, and each card showed one example of a Spanish word with its English translation. She would distribute two sets of these cards at random to the class, so that each word was given to two students. However, the complete vocabulary list with English equivalents was not visible on the board at the front; only the students with a card could see the word on it. As it was a class of thirty students there were some students without cards.

The teacher then called out one of the words on the cards, for example, *triste*. This was a cue for those two students who had been given the card with *triste* to stand up and shout out the Spanish and the English '*triste* – sad'. The student who said it first was the winner.

I could see how engaged the students were who had been given the word. I wanted to change the activity so that more students were involved and also so that more vocabulary could be covered, because I was not keen on the idea of some students sitting passively. After all, the following section in the current Ofsted framework for school inspection clearly states: '175. The most important role of teaching is to promote learning and the acquisition of knowledge by pupils and to raise achievement.'[1] No one could ever argue

---

[1] Ofsted, (2015).

against this. But how can *all* students' achievement needs be met if not all of them are participating?

I am in no way criticising that excellent teacher who used this activity but I did want to find a more productive way of involving more of the students with more vocabulary. I thought I could do this by:

- preparing a longer list of vocabulary or phrases
- numbering the list (as in the figure)
- dividing the class into halves to create two teams competing against each other
- appointing a captain for each team who could give out the numbers to the other students

I bought a set of football-captain armbands and a collection of sports trophies which I had engraved with 'Language Champion' (these worked especially well with boys). As a consequence, the students in the group were more motivated to give out the numbers of the words to the other students and to try to win the trophy for their side of the class.

The first time I tried this VFLA was with a Year 7 group. I used it as my plenary in the lesson with short basic sentences describing hair and eye colour in the Target Language with the English translation next to each. On a PowerPoint slide I typed out thirteen Target Language sentences, such as:

1. *J'ai les cheveux blonds.* = I have blond hair.
2. *J'ai les yeux verts.* = I have green eyes.

Once the student captains had given out all of the numbers to their team I explained that I would randomly call out the number of a sentence on the slide projected on the board and whichever student had been assigned that number would then 'Bob-Up' out of their seat and call out the word in both the Target Language and in English. The quickest student on either side to say this would win the point for their side.

I discovered this was effective for practising knowledge imparted earlier in the lesson and also for retrieval practice. By showing students slides with either *just* the Target Language or *just* the English (you will need to prepare two slides with these options beforehand), you can then have the students bobbing up and calling out both terms. This provides a random test of their knowledge which is not shown when they are competing against each other with both the Target Language and English showing.

It works with all year groups, but with older groups I would focus explicitly and with good humour on the competitive nature of the VFLA. Be assertive and tell the students that they can't let their team down so they all have to have a number and be involved.

Remember that this is not something frivolous but rather a way to practise vocabulary and short phrases with the aim of making it stick.

I wouldn't use any of the VFLAs at the beginning of the lesson with a group I had just begun teaching. Like any innovation, the key is to introduce it gradually and create a routine. For one group my routine through the entire academic year was to practise Bob-Up Classic in the last ten minutes with a trusted student keeping a tally-chart of the winners.

Preparation and resources

- Identify the group of Target Language words or phrases that you want to practise with a class (there is an example on page 37 and many more at www.crownhouse. co.uk/featured/fun-mfl). Copy the vocabulary or phrases onto a PowerPoint slide and number each item.
- Arrange your classroom seating plan so you can divide the class into halves.
- Project the vocabulary or phrases onto the board so that every student can see them.

Instructions

- Ask for or choose two student captains to represent their side. Give them a captain's armband each.
- Tell the class that the captains have thirty seconds to give out the numbers (or the words) for the words on the PowerPoint slide projected on the board to all the students in their team.
- Once they have their number they must write down in their books the word or words projected onto the board.
- If there are more numbers on the slide than there are students on each side then some students will have to have more than one number (and therefore more than one word).
- Stand at the front of the class and call out any number (or word) in English or in the Target Language. The first student to bob up and say both the Target Language and the English phrase corresponding to the number you have called out wins a point for their side.
- Award a mark to the winning team.
- Quickly call out another number and repeat the process.

Variations to the VFLA

- Test the students' retrieval by asking them to write their *own* list of vocabulary or phrases that they have learned in the lesson, and project this list for Bob-Up Classic.
- Project either a slide of just the Target Language or a slide of just the English, then call out a number and see which students can bob up, say the word(s) for that number and then give the English meaning.

Teacher notes

Vary when you conduct Bob-Up Classic. Once a class is familiar with how it works, use it at any point during the lesson. Tell the students to swap numbers with the person next to them so as to ensure that students practise different vocabulary.

Ideally, the students will know how to pronounce the words you use as you will have already modelled the pronunciation. However, there may still be students who ask how to pronounce the word or phrase. If so, that's great because it means they're thinking about their word: they want to pronounce it correctly for their team. Any way that you can get the students thinking about the words they are saying is going to help them to remember their meanings. As Willingham says, 'Whatever you think about, that's what you remember.'[2]

---

[2] Willingham, (2009) p. 61.

**Here's a vocab list in Spanish to get you started
(also available at www.crownhouse.co.uk/featured/fun-mfl)**

1. *desde hace* + verb in present tense = to have been (and still be) doing something (*vivo aquí desde hace cinco años* = I've been living here for five years)
2. *compartir una habitación/un dormitorio* = to share a room
3. *ruidoso* = noisy   *ruido* = noise
4. *partido* = match (football, tennis, etc.)
5. *equitación* = horse-riding   *montar a caballo* = to go horse-riding
6. *hacer vela* = sailing
7. *piragüismo* = canoeing
8. *primavera* = spring   *verano* = summer   *otoño* = autumn   *invierno* = winter
9. *triste* = sad
10. *país* = country
11. *sensible* = sensitive
12. *tengo que* + infinitive = I have to …
13. *asco* = disgust   *asqueroso* = disgusting
14. *hace* + time phrase = ago   (*hace cuatro años* = four years ago)
15. *conocer* = to know BUT *conocer a* = to meet (someone) OR to get to know (someone)
16. *novio/novia* = boyfriend / girlfriend
17. *hacer amigos* AND *hacer amistades* = to make friends   *amistad* = friendship
    amistoso AND *amable* = friendly
18. *en el extranjero* = abroad
19. *peligroso* = dangerous   *peligro* = danger
20. *joven* = young   *juventud* = youth
21. *casarse/se casaron / se casó / casamiento/casado* = ALL TO DO WITH GETTING MARRIED
    boda = wedding
22. *salud* = health   *sano* = healthy (person)   *saludable* = healthy (food, etc.)
23. *cocinero* = cook
24. *desayuno* = breakfast
25. *enfermo* = ill
26. *demasiado* = too   (*demasiado* is a common 'trick' in a positive-or-negative type
    question: *demasiado tranquilo* = too peaceful)   *demasiados/demasiadas* = too many

2 Random (VFLA)

On the strength of the success of Bob-Up Classic I started thinking more about the characteristics of language games I had come across, especially about the importance of displaying as much vocabulary as possible.

One drawback to Bob-Up Classic, even though the whole class is involved, is that only one or two vocabulary items were assigned to each student. Whilst one student could swap words with another, I wanted another way to make the process of showing students words and saying the Target Language and the English as competitive as possible.

So, if I just projected a long list of numbered vocabulary without assigning any of the numbers to the students and simply stood next to the board, then I could randomly call out the Target Language or the English for any of the words on the list. Because no words are assigned to anyone, any student is free to bob up and say either the English translation if I call out the Target Language or say the Target Language translation if I call out the English. The student who bobs up and calls the Target Language *and* the English meaning first wins a point for their team. This is rapid fire and a simple, competitive and effective way of 'warming the words up'. Other ways of assigning meaning to the vocabulary are described in Vlotto (VFLA #12).

Preparation and resources

- Identify the group of Target Language words or phrases that you want to practise with a class. This could be a list of key vocabulary such as the example on page 41 and there are many more at www.crownhouse.co.uk/featured/fun-mfl. Copy the vocabulary or phrases onto a PowerPoint slide and number each item.
- Arrange your classroom seating plan so that you can divide the class into halves.
- Project the vocabulary or phrases onto the board so that every student can see the language.

Instructions

- Explain that you are going to say the Target Language word *or* the English meaning for any of the words projected on the board.
- As soon as a student identifies the word you've called out they bob up and say it along with the English or Target Language translation.
- The first student to do this wins the point for their side. Keep a tally of points won on the whiteboard.
- Then call a different Target Language word or English meaning out and the process is repeated.
- The VFLA continues like this until one side has scored ten points.

Variations to the VFLA

- The same variations work as with Bob-Up Classic: discuss with the students which words they have learned in the lesson and project these.
- If students aren't bobbing up, change what they have to do before calling out the Target Language and English. For example, buy some cheap buzzers for them to use. (You might think they're gimmicky, but students talk about such classroom experiences and it may even go viral! And this type of gimmick can help build a relationship and culture with these same students later in the academic year, just as the names of the VFLAs do. You refer back to earlier lessons saying, 'Remember when we had those buzzers? Remember the first time that I used those in class? What was the first bit of vocab you picked out with your buzzer on that slide?')

I once bought a set of sixteen hotel reception bells and used these with a class with the Random VFLA. Instead of the students bobbing up and calling out, they rang the bells and called out. It's hardly ground-breaking technology but it certainly had an effect. I also used them with the Boards, Bells and Textbook Tasks FLA #13 (you may have guessed that!).

Although I wouldn't recommend using these props in the first few lessons you have with a class, having a bell, buzzer or whistle here and there can be a potentially useful behaviour management technique that paradoxically gets a noisy class to be silent.[3] Just don't overuse them; ensure that ultimately the focus is always on the learning. The use is justified when a student pops a question out of the blue like, 'Can we use the bells again?'

Teacher notes

There is always a danger that the same students will dominate this VFLA. If this is a problem tell the dominating students that the next time they call out a word they then have to call out the name of another student, who has to repeat the Target Language and English. Point out that the dominating student cannot call out the same name more than once.

With a smaller group, if you feel the students are 'bobbed-up out', tell them that they can just call out the words without bobbing up.

Competitiveness keeps things moving very fast. The students are keen to gain points for their side.

Remember to discuss the meaning of some of the words from time to time, before starting again or testing retrieval. Make it fast and pacy, make it competitive, make the words mean something to the students, test them.

---

[3] M. R. Major, (2008) *The Teacher's Survival Guide: Real Classroom Dilemmas and Practical Solutions*, Lanham, MD, Rowman & Littlefield Education. p. 266.

**Here's a vocab list in French to get you started
(also available at www.crownhouse.co.uk/featured/fun–mfl)**

1. *conducteur* AND *chauffeur* = driver   *conduire* = to drive
2. *bruit* = noise   *bruyant* = noisy
3. *planche à voile* = windsurfing   *voile* = sailing
4. *plongée* = diving
5. *il n'y a que* = there is / are only (*ne … que* = only)
6. *partager* = to share
7. *il est interdit de/il est défendu de* + infinitive = it is forbidden to …
8. *jours de congé* = days off   *jours fériés* = public holidays
9. *lait solaire* = sun cream   *coup de soleil* = sunstroke
10. *tranquille* = quiet   *paisible* = peaceful
11. *escrime* = fencing
12. *se défouler/se détendre/se relâcher/se reposer* = to relax / rest
    détente/repos = relaxation / rest
13. *s'évader de/s'échapper de* = to escape from   *éviter* = to avoid
14. *histoire* = history OR story
15. *l'écran* = screen   (*le petit écran* = TV)   *les places* = (cinema) seats / places
16. *accueillir* = to welcome   *bienvenue* = welcome
17. *drôle* = funny   *fidèle* = loyal   *fiable* = reliable
18. *le film paraît/semble* = the film seems
19. *enseignant* = teacher   *instituteur/institutrice* = primary school teacher
20. *beau-père/beau-frère* = father-in-law / brother-in-law
    belle-mère/belle-sœur = mother-in-law / sister-in-law
21. *fonctionnaires* = civil servants
22. *équipe* = team   *sports d'equipe* = team sports
23. *ambiance* = atmosphere
24. *bras* = arm   *jambe* = leg   *bouche* = mouth   *gorge* = throat   *doigt* = finger
    main = hand   *pied* = foot   *genou* = knee   *cheville* = ankle
    estomac/ventre = stomach   *yeux* = eyes   *œil* = eye   *oreilles* = ears   *tête* = head
    dents = teeth   *dos* = back   *épaule* = shoulder   *ongles* = nails

3 Random Random (VFLA)

This VFLA involves students in a story told by the teacher, in which they have to solve a problem.

I devised Random Random because I wanted a way of making certain words more memorable. Students are more likely to remember words once they have thought about their meaning. To this end, I projected a list of key vocabulary on the board such as the example on page 45. I chose a word from the projected list but did not share this with the students. Instead, I told a story related to the word's meaning.

For example, let's say that I have chosen *Regen* (rain). I might start by saying, 'The other day I went for a walk into the mountains, but I had some problems getting to the summit as I had to do a lot of walking, and the weather was not great … ' and so on, carefully avoiding the word 'rain' but giving clues, both pertinent and misleading.

Whenever the students think they know the word that I am telling a story about, they bob up and call out the Target Language word and the English translation. They are free to bob up and guess the word at any point. I only stop telling my story after a student has correctly identified the word my story refers to. If a student bobs up and calls out '*Regenmantel*, raincoat!' I just continue my story – until a student bobs up and correctly calls out '*Regen*, rain!'

This results in a classroom of students scanning the list of projected words and randomly bobbing up, calling out words from the projected slide while trying to match the meaning of the words to my story. Once the word has been guessed, I award a point to that side and I start the process again by choosing a different word.

When I first introduced this the students treated it more like a gap-filling exercise. They expected me to pause so that they could bob up and call out the Target Language to complete the sentence. For instance, imagine I'm telling a story based on the vocabulary on page 45: 'So, I went to the restaurant last night with my friends and we had a lot of … ' When I stop telling the story the students bob up and call out a word they think fills the gap in the sentence; for example, '*Spaß*, fun!' However, by deliberately keeping the story vague or ambiguous, you can trick students into guessing incorrect words; you as the storyteller can be unpredictable by changing the story, adding the odd twist and turn and by giving students red herrings.

Even when guessing words and getting them wrong, the students are still calling out meanings for other words on the list. When a Target Language word and English meaning are called out by a student guessing, the rest of the class are still being reminded of that meaning.

The process is again rapid fire. The whole class gets involved as they focus on the list of vocabulary projected onto the board, and pay attention to the story the teacher is telling. *Random* students guessing with a *random* story gives you Random Random.

Preparation and resources

- Identify the group of Target Language words or phrases that you want to practise with a class (there is an example on page 45 and many more at www.crownhouse.co.uk/featured/fun-mfl). Copy the words and phrases onto a PowerPoint slide.
- You don't have to number the words for this VFLA but as the slide may be used with other VFLAs, you can leave the numbers on.
- Arrange your classroom seating plan so that you can divide the class into halves.
- Project the vocabulary or phrases onto the board so that every student can see them.

Instructions

If the class is not familiar with the VFLA you might have to explain that it is not a 'gap-filling' activity.

- Tell the class that you are going to think of a Target Language word which is on the PowerPoint slide projected on the board, but you are not going to tell them which it is.
- Explain that you are going to tell a story in English (or the Target Language if appropriate to the level of ability) related to this word or phrase, and that whenever any student thinks they know which word you are referring to in your story, they have to bob up and call out the Target Language and the English for this.

- If the student guesses correctly then you will award a point to their team.
- They are free to bob up and call out the Target Language and English at any point during your story, but you will only stop telling your story once a student has called out the correct Target Language and English word.

Variations to the VFLA

- At a higher level, tell the story in the Target Language. This has worked well at A level with the students also having to explain in the Target Language why they called out the word they did.
- Instead of the teacher, get a student from each team or side of the class to tell the story. The student captain on each side could nominate the student to tell the story.

Teacher notes

Students must all be focused, looking at the projected list of vocabulary and not at their classmates or the storyteller. The teacher has to monitor that all students are scanning the list of projected vocabulary while the story is being told.

**Here's a vocab list in German to get you started
(also available at www.crownhouse.co.uk/featured/fun-mfl)**

1. *Teilzeitjob* = part-time job
2. *leicht* = easy
3. *arbeitslos* = unemployed   *Mitarbeiter* = colleague
4. *Kunde/Kundin* = customer
5. *beliebt* = popular
6. *Kellner/Kellnerin* = waiter/waitress   BUT *Kerl* = chap
7. *Berufsschule* = vocational school/college   *Beruf* = occupation/career
8. *Gäste* = guests
9. *Trinkgeld* = tip (money)   *Taschengeld* = pocket money
   Geld zurück = change/money back
10. *sparen* = to save (money)
11. *großzügig* = generous
12. *Urlaub* = holiday (*im Urlaub* = on holiday)   *Ferien* = holidays
    (*in den Ferien* = during the holidays)   *Sommerferien* = summer holidays
13. *besonders* = especially
14. *Oberstufe* = 6th form/upper school   *Mitschüler* = classmate
    Grundschule = primary school   *Lehrer/Lehrerin* = teacher   *Fach* = school subject
15. *schwer* AND *schwierig* = difficult   *Unterricht* = lessons   (*im Unterricht* = in lessons)
16. *Lehrerzimmer* = staffroom   *Abitur* = A levels   *Aufgabe* = job/task
    Realschule = high school
17. *leider* = unfortunately
18. *doof* AND *dumm* AND *blöd* = stupid   *Dummheit* = stupidity   *Blödsinn* = nonsense
19. *Wald* = forest
20. *schön* = pleasant OR beautiful
21. *Spaß* = fun   *es hat Spaß gemacht* = it was/has been fun
    sich amüsieren = to enjoy oneself
22. *Lieder* = songs
23. *heute* = today   *heutzutage* = nowadays   *nun* AND *jetzt* = now
24. *früh* = early   *spät* = late   *zu spät* = too late
25. *morgen* = tomorrow OR morning   *nachmittags* = in the afternoon   *täglich* = daily
26. *Regen* = rain   *Regenmantel* = raincoat
27. *Lust haben + zu* = to want to ...   *Lust haben + auf* = to want/feel like (something)

4 Mexican Wave (VFLA)

I often use the Mexican Wave to kick off vocabulary practice. Coming into class and shouting out 'Mexican Wave!' with a class already trained on the ins and outs (or in this case, its ups and downs) makes for a powerful, fast-paced start to the lesson. You might use the Mexican Wave to inject a dollop of *oomph* to help cure the Monday morning blues. It's a great rapport builder too. However, remember it's not just a *fun* activity. As David Didau says, you don't want to be in a position where students are thinking solely about all the fun they're having rather than thinking about the vocabulary.[4]

The students, in their rows, rise in turn, do a Mexican Wave and say the Target Language and English word projected on the board. As they sit back down, the next student immediately does the same with the next vocabulary item on the projected list, and so on down the line. Both sides do this simultaneously; the team that finishes first wins. The Wave should be a smooth succession of rising, waving, speaking and sitting, rising, waving, speaking and sitting until … 'Left side wins!'

After a round or two, before switching to another VFLA, take a moment to get students thinking about the meaning of the vocabulary they have just 'Mexican Waved'. Talk about the most difficult words to say, discover the students' favourite sounding words, ask them what their top three favourite words are on the slide. Then move on.

---

4   David Didau, (2013) 'The Problem with Fun', *Learning Spy* (blog). See http://www.learningspy.co.uk/education/the-problem-with-fun/.

Preparation and resources

- Identify the group of Target Language words or phrases that you want to practise with a class (there is an example on page 48 and many more at www.crownhouse.co.uk/featured/fun-mfl). Copy the vocabulary onto a PowerPoint slide and number each item.
- Arrange your classroom seating plan so that the class is divided into halves with the students aligned in rows.
- Project the vocabulary or phrases onto the board so that every student can see them.

Instructions

- Tell the class that this VFLA is a race activity with one side of the class versus the other.
- The student at the end of the row nearest the board on each side begins, followed in order by their neighbour, and so on, to the end of the line. As this is a race, students should be doing the Mexican Wave and speaking more quickly than those on the other side.
- When you say the Target Language cue-word for 'go' the first student bobs up, does a Mexican Wave and says the first Target Language word at the top of the list and its English translation and sits back down.
- Immediately after the first student is seated again, the next student bobs up, does the wave, and says the second Target Language word and English on the projected list.
- The Mexican Wave is complete when the last student in the line has sat down again. The first side to do this wins the point.

Variations to the VFLA

- Start with the student sat at the back on each side beginning the wave.
- Start one side off from the student sat at the back while at the same time start the other side off from the student sat at the front and then see who wins.
- A 'class versus the clock' approach works quite well with the whole class. Start the wave off so just one student bobs up, does the wave and speaks the first projected Target Language and English meaning of the vocabulary, then the student sitting next to them does the same, followed by the next student and so on around the class. When the last student completes the wave you stop the clock. Make a note of the time and run it again to see if 'your class team' can beat this time.
- Get the class to do the wave so that every row is competing against each other row. Go along the row, or there and back, one or more times. The first row to complete this win the point for their side and should then write down their five favourite words with the other rows doing the same once they complete the list.

Teacher notes

If you have an odd number of students, run the Mexican Wave as above but when the wave reaches the last student on the shorter side the wave goes into reverse for one student.

Once a side has won the Mexican Wave, a good VFLA to use before testing retrieval is Random Random (VFLA #3). It works well as a way of attaching a meaning to words that have just been 'rapidly fired'.

Here's a vocab list in German to get you started
(also available at www.crownhouse.co.uk/featured/fun-mfl)

1. *leiden* = to stand/bear OR to suffer
2. *Sendung* = programme   (*Jugendsendung* = youth programme)
3. *Verhältnis* = relationship
4. *Zuschauer* = spectator(s)/viewer(s)
5. *Nachrichten* = news   *Zeitung* = newspaper
6. *Lippenstift* = lipstick   *Ohrringe* = earrings
7. *Gepäck* = luggage   *Koffer* = suitcase
8. *gut/schlecht gelaunt* = in a good/bad mood   *Laune* = mood
9. *Wettbewerb* = competition
10. *Schmuck* = jewellery   *Spielzeug* = toys
11. *Dosen* = tins/cans
12. *Schultasche* = schoolbag
13. *Heizung* = heating
14. *Schlips* = tie
15. *Gewicht* = weight   *Übergewicht haben* = to be overweight
16. *Fernseher* = TV (set)
17. *Zwillingsschwester* = twin sister   *Zwillingsbruder* = twin brother
18. *Recht haben* = to be right
19. *Strom* = current (water/electricity)
20. *überlegen* = to consider   *berichten* = to report
21. *neulich* = recently
22. *gucken* = to watch   *Fernsehen gucken* = to watch TV
23. *Werbung* = advertising   *Trickfilm* = animated cartoon/film
24. *während* = while OR during
25. *sowieso* = anyway/in any case
26. *Seifenopern* = soap operas
27. *turnen* = to do gymnastics

5 Toy Time (VFLA)

The Toy Time VFLA takes place in groups of four with a soft toy being passed amongst group members. A soft toy should be a regular feature in any language teacher's locker!

As an erstwhile Year 7 language learner, the initiation-response-feedback technique (IRF) always involved flashcards. Jones and Wiliam mention this in *Modern Foreign Languages: Inside the Black Box*[5] with reference to Sinclair and Coulthard's study of classroom discourse (1975), where the teacher asks questions such as, '*Qu'est-ce que c'est?*' and the student answers, '*C'est un chat,*' followed by the teacher feeding back that it was indeed a cat, '*Oui, c'est un chat,*' before moving on.

However, once Over Head Projectors (OHPs) and transparencies became *à la mode* the soft toy made a regular appearance in lessons as the teacher put the flashcards down but still continued the IRF technique by throwing the toy to a student, asking the *qu'est-ce que c'est?* question while pointing to a projected image of a dog, cat, mouse, or whatever, projected onto the board. The student receiving the toy would give the *c'est un chien* answer before throwing it back to the teacher, who then gave the *oui, c'est un chien* feedback as above. And so on round the classroom with a variety of different pictures. Sometimes, instead of (often poorly drawn) images on a transparency the teacher would simply stick a range of flashcards on the board and then carry out the IRF technique armed with the toy. (If you listened carefully, 'I'm a

---

[5] J. Jones and D. Wiliam, (2008) *Modern Foreign Languages: Inside the Black Box*, Chiswick, GL Assessment. p. 6.

languages teacher, not an art teacher!' could occasionally be heard in the Modern Languages corner of the staffroom.)

The soft toy is a useful device, even in these hi-tech days, and the last thing that we should be doing is leaving it on top of a pile of transparencies in the storeroom. Instead of directing proceedings at the front, throwing a soft toy about to individual students and practising the IRF technique, you're giving each group in the class a toy and letting them get on with it.

Preparation and resources

- Identify the group of Target Language words or phrases that you want to practise with a class (there is an example on page 52 and many more at www.crownhouse. co.uk/featured/fun-mfl). Copy the vocabulary or phrases onto a PowerPoint slide and number each item.
- Arrange your classroom seating plan to divide the class into three or four rows on each side of the classroom.
- Do a countdown and shout 'go' in the Target Language.
- Project the vocabulary or phrases onto the board so that every student can see them.
- Hand out a toy to the student at the end of each row. Once the VFLA is underway, observe the students in their rows speaking the vocabulary in turn while passing the toy.

Instructions

- Explain that the class are going to work in their rows of three or four and that they must look at the projected vocabulary list on the board.
- The first student on each row will have a toy which they will be passing to each other and saying the vocabulary.
- The first student says all the Target Language and English for number one on the projected list. They then pass the toy to the student next to them who does the same for number two on the list, and so on.
- The toy moves back and forth along the row until the students have reached the bottom. The first row in the class to do this all bob up to show that they have won, and win a point.

Variations to the VFLA

- Vary the starting point: run it from the top of the list and then shout out, 'From the bottom!' Shout this out in Target Language if the group are well trained.

- Get one student to say the Target Language and the other student to say the English meaning for it.
- Get one student to say the Target Language word, and spell the word using the Target Language alphabet, followed by the other student saying the English meaning.
- Project an irregular verb table onto the board.
- Add some action! (Again, not for the faint-hearted!) Each student has to bob up to say the Target Language vocab and English meaning, and sit down again, before the turn passes to the other student. (I tried this once as part of a cross-curricular MFL PE lesson with students doing a circuit routine where one student was doing a press-up or sit-up while the other student called out the Target Language word and English from a handout; then they swapped. This kind of thing certainly creates a buzz and gets students talking about language lessons.)

Teacher notes

Discuss the meaning of vocabulary after the winning row has been decided before varying practice with another VFLA or testing retrieval. Ask two or three students to give you their favourite sounding three words, and so on.

Here's a vocab list in Spanish to get you started
(also available at www.crownhouse.co.uk/featured/fun-mfl)

1. *merendar* = to snack
2. *perezoso* AND *vago* = lazy   *orgulloso* = proud
3. *descansar* = to rest
4. *amarillear* = to turn yellow
5. *delgado* = thin   *adelgazar* = to get thinner OR to slim   *perder peso* = to lose weight
6. *evitar* = to avoid
7. *alimento* = food
8. *gordo* = fat   *engordar* = to get fatter
9. *grasa* = fat   *sal* = salt   *azúcar* = sugar   *comida rápida/basura* = fast/junk food
10. *correr* = to run   *hacer footing* = to go jogging
11. *diariamente* = daily
12. *estar en forma* = to be fit   *mantenerse en forma* = to keep fit
13. *platos* = dishes   (*platos con grasa* = fatty dishes)
14. *refresco* = soft drink
15. *pulmones* = lungs   *hígado* = liver
16. *emborracharse* = to get drunk   *borracho* = drunk
17. *sustancias* = substances   *altos niveles de* = high levels of
    drogas blandas/duras = soft/hard drugs
18. *riesgos* = risks
19. *sida* = AIDS
20. *casado* = married BUT *cansado* = tired/tiring   *agotado* = exhausted
    agotador = exhausting
21. *padres* = parents BUT *parientes* = relatives
22. *al aire libre* = in the open air   *aire puro* = pure air
23. *leer* = to read   *lectura* = reading
24. *enseñar* = to teach/show   *enseñanza* = education/teaching
25. *aumentar/incrementar/subir* = to increase/go up
    aumento/incremento/subida = increase
    descender/bajar = to decrease/go down   *descenso* = decrease
26. *extranjero* = foreign   *idioma* = language
    idioma extranjero OR *lengua extranjera* = foreign language
27. *países* = countries   *países extranjeros* = foreign countries
    países del Tercer Mundo = Third World countries
28. *aprender* = to learn   *fracaso escolar* = failure at school

6 Vocab Piler (VFLA)

This VFLA is not quite as rapid fire as others and gives more control to the students. It is essentially a survey, completed by the students, on vocabulary chosen from a list projected on the board. A survey is an effective means of getting the students to practise language independently from the teacher.

It takes longer than many of the other VFLAs and there are a number of steps needed for carrying it out effectively.

The Vocab Piler works in a similar way to other kinds of survey. The students ask each other a key question or a list of questions, and note down the responses. They then move on to another student and do the same. However, instead of questions and answers as in a survey, this is pure vocab, vocab, vocab …

In *Debates in Modern Languages Education* the notion of self-created vocabulary lists are referred to as 'another important way in which learners can visualise and measure their progress'.[6] Although not created quite as naturally as described in *Debates*, this is what the Vocab Piler is all about: students generate their own vocabulary lists through an engaging activity in which they compile a list of words that they don't know, based on the list projected on the board and what their classmates say.

---

[6] Driscoll et al., (2014) p. 75.

The students look at the list, choosing six words they didn't know the meaning of and writing them down (Target Language and English meaning). They rate each word from one to six according to their favourite and least preferred. They then conduct a survey with each other. They say their list to another student who notes down any words not on their list *and* which they do not know the meaning of. The result is a class of students with a long list of words that they did not know the meaning of at the start. The Vocab Piler is rooted in students deciding for themselves which word meanings they add to their list and which they don't.

Preparation and resources

- Identify the group of Target Language words or phrases that you want to practise with a class. For example, this could be a list of key vocabulary (there is an example on page 56 and many more at www.crownhouse.co.uk/featured/fun-mfl) which includes words that are new or known to be challenging. Copy the vocabulary or phrases onto a PowerPoint slide. There is no need to number each item, but you might as well because you can run other VFLAs with the same list.
- Arrange your classroom seating plan so that you can divide the class into halves.
- Project the vocabulary or phrases onto the board so that every student can see them.

Instructions

Part one

- Tell the students to choose and write down six Target Language words and their meanings from the list projected onto the board.
- Ask them to rate each word on a scale of one to six according to how much they like each one. Tell them to write the numbers 1 to 6 next to each word with 1 being their favourite word and 6 being their least favourite.
- When you say the Target Language phrase for 'go' they stand up, find the student nearest to them and take turns to speak their list of six vocabulary items in the order they rated them (in the Target Language and English).
- The listener can ask the speaker to repeat this list as many times as they like.
- The listener writes down any words they have heard which they do not know the meaning of *and* which are not already on their own list of six.
- The students then reverse roles.
- Once a pair of students has completed this process they find another pair of students and follow the same process with them. Explain that each student only says their own original list of six each time but that they should be adding extra vocabulary and phrases that they don't know the meaning of that the new partner tells them.
- Run the Vocab Piler for ten minutes.

Part two

- Stop the survey after the time limit and ask the students to sit down.
- Tell the class that you want them to now rate their *new* list of words according to their favourite and least favourite just as they did with their original list of six.
- The students work in pairs with each student making a list of *just* the English or *just* the Target Language of *their partner's whole list* of vocabulary (the original six Target Language words and meanings and any extras accumulated during the survey).
- Turn off the list of words on the board, and ask the students to give the list of just the English or just the Target Language to their partner and get the students to complete the list from memory.
- The students mark the number of words they got right (checking against their original list).
- Finally, get the students to celebrate their vocabulary gains by calling out, telling their partner, writing down on the MWB on the walls, sticky notes on walls, etc. the number of vocabulary items they *now* know. Tell the students to make a note of this as their personal best for the Vocab Piler VFLA.

Variations to the VFLA

- Vary the number of Target Language words and English meanings that you want the students to write down at the start of the process.
- Vary the time limit you allow for the survey.

Teacher notes

This VFLA requires some practice before the students can follow the process exactly. Once a class is familiar with it, though, the vocabulary gains can be immense and the students enjoy practising the vocabulary independently from the teacher directing VFLA proceedings.

It is a useful VFLA for introducing a change in pace in vocabulary practice. Willingham suggests, 'plan shifts and monitor your class's attention to see whether you need to make them more often or less frequently'.[7]

The pronunciation of the words needs to have been clearly modelled first as the class will be speaking their list again and again. Also, this VFLA works better with a large list of vocabulary to start with.

---

[7] Willingham, (2009) p. 22.

The competition element of this VFLA is not about sides versus sides, but about students competing with themselves to see how many vocabulary *gains* they can make in a lesson; each student is improving their personal best.

Here's a vocab list in French to get you started (also available at www.crownhouse.co.uk/featured/fun-mfl)

1. *entreprise* = company
2. *s'inquiéter* = to worry
3. *les gens n'utilisent plus* = people no longer use (*ne … plus* = no longer)
4. *chômage* = unemployment   *chômeurs* = the unemployed
5. *immeuble* = block of flats
6. *espoir* = hope
7. *santé* = health   *sain* = healthy
8. *j'ai tort* = I'm wrong   *j'ai raison* = I'm right
9. *il/elle est né(e)* = he / she was born   *je suis né(e)* = I was born   *naissance* = birth
   (*date de naissance* = date of birth)   (*lieu de naissance* = place of birth)
10. *publicité/pub* = advertising
11. *de mauvaise/bonne humeur* = in a bad / good mood
12. *s'entraîner* = to train   *faire la queue* = to queue up
13. *célèbre* = famous
14. *se promener/faire une promenade/se balader/marcher* = ALL TO DO WITH WALKING
    faire une randonnée = to go for a hike
15. *marcher* = to work (function)   (*ça ne marche pas* = it doesn't work / it isn't working)
16. *je suis devenu(e)* = I became   (*devenir* = to become)
17. *patinage/patiner/patin à glace/patinoire* = ALL TO DO WITH ICE-SKATING
18. *s'amuser* = to have fun   *distractions* = entertainment
19. *bricolage* = DIY   *en bois* = (made of) wood   *en pierre* = (made of) stone
    en laine = (made of) wool   *en cuir* = (made of) leather
20. *étranger* = foreign OR abroad   *étrangers* = foreigners OR strangers
21. *trajet* = journey
22. *éviter* = to avoid
23. *mal à l'aise* = ill at ease
24. *banlieue* = suburbs   *environs/alentours* = outskirts / surroundings
25. *jeter* = to throw away   *jeter des papiers* = to litter
26. *argent de poche* = pocket money   *compte* (*bancaire*) = (bank) account
    somme = amount (of money)

7 Blaster (VFLA)

The Blaster VFLA is not for the faint-hearted! The idea is simple: it's all about speed. The teacher projects the vocabulary slide onto the board and each student simultaneously says out loud the Target Language words or phrases with the English meaning, going from top to bottom of the slide. The first student to reach the bottom bobs up and is the winner.

Its simplicity means that it works extremely well as a last-minute *massed practice* strategy; for example, in the run-up to a GCSE reading or listening exam. This is most definitely rapid fire stuff, hence the name Blaster.

However, the VFLA comes with a warning. A trainee teacher once witnessed me using this with a class and saw its impact when I used it alongside other VFLAs and then tested retrieval. This VFLA works very well with a class who have been *trained* to do it. When the trainee teacher tried it with a class in her following placement not all students responded as well as she had hoped. Indeed, when I tried it in the first or second lesson with a class at a new school, it was oddly received. Why? Because the atmosphere of fun and almost self-mocking competition had not yet been established between class and teacher; the rapport was lacking.

Once students have been trained on the importance of the VFLA they know they have to say the words properly and not skip any words on the list. If you find students 'cheating', stop the activity, explain that this is not what you expect and restart it correctly. Use the fun, competitive element but focus ultimately on the goal. Once the philosophy behind the VFLAs has been established and a relationship built with the class, the Blaster VFLA can easily be sold to a class on the premise of competition and humour. Telling a class that everyone has to call out the projected words from top to bottom as fast they can may seem a little crazy or chaotic, but as long as you are insistent on the fact that everyone is going to do it to see who wins and joke that whoever does win becomes Blaster Champion, then the Blaster VFLA can be a vital part of your knowledge-imparting and knowledge-practising armoury.

Towards the end of her placement, the trainee teacher was using the Blaster with a number of her classes, as was I in my new school. As Doug Lemov comments: 'The finest teachers offer up their work with generous servings of energy, passion, enthusiasm, fun, and humor.'[8]

Another key part of this VFLA is what you do when the winner has finished, before doing another VFLA or practising retrieval. Immediately after the Blaster, what works well (as with the other VFLAs) is to ask the students which words were the most difficult to say, which words they liked the sound of best, or to rank four or five words according to some criterion. All these strategies encourage the students to think about the list of words they have just spoken and help them focus on meaning.

Preparation and resources

- Identify the group of Target Language words or phrases that you want to practise with a class (there is an example on page 60 and many more at www.crownhouse. co.uk/featured/fun-mfl). Copy the vocabulary or phrases onto a PowerPoint slide and number each item.
- Arrange your classroom seating plan so that you can divide the class into two.
- Project the vocabulary or phrases onto the board so that every student can see them.

Instructions

- Explain to the class that they are going to do a Blaster, but first you are going to model it: you call out the Target Language words and English as fast as you can from the first word on the list down to the last.
- You then do a countdown in the Target Language and when you say 'go' everyone is going to do as you have just done: say out loud the Target Language words and phrases and English on the slide, from top to bottom.

---

[8] Lemov, (2010) p. 214.

- This is a competition. Everyone must say all the words, so no skipping (otherwise the VFLA will be abandoned and negative consequences ensue!). The first student to reach the last word or phrase has to bob up to show they have won.
- Put a tally mark on the board for the side with the student who won the Blaster.

Variations to the VFLA

- Students start from the bottom of the projected vocabulary list and work their way up to the top.
- Switch VFLAs midway through the list: students complete the first ten words from the list as a Blaster then the second ten as Toy Time (VFLA #5) with their partner sitting next to them.
- Instead of competing against each other as individuals within sides, buy a countdown clock (such as a Kagan MegaTimer™) and get the class competing against the clock.

Teacher notes

Familiarise the class with this VFLA by asking for a student volunteer to do the Blaster first. Having a more confident student doing this helps create a more relaxed classroom.

Remember that whilst the winner of the Blaster can be championed, winning Blaster is not a measure of language ability. The mindset for this VFLA is challenge. Lemov reminds us that kids love to be challenged. This doesn't just mean going up against the other team; they can also compete against their personal standards, such as a previous time or test-score, or just to prove to others that they can do it.[9]

---

[9] Lemov, (2010) p. 208.

Here's a vocab list in German to get you started
(also available at www.crownhouse.co.uk/featured/fun-mfl)

1. *Lokal* = premises OR bar
2. *gemütlich* = cosy / comfortable   *bequem* = comfortable   *(un)angenehm* = (un)pleasant
3. *sondern* = but rather
4. *Gebäck* = biscuits   *Süßwaren* AND *Süßigkeiten* = sweets   *lecker* = tasty / delicious
5. *Wirt* = landlord   *Wirtshaus* = pub / inn   *Gastgeber* = host
6. *Rezept* = recipe OR prescription
7. *stammen aus* = to come from
8. *Geschichte* = history OR story
9. *wandern* = to hike   *Wanderung* = hike   *spazieren gehen* = to go for a walk
   Spaziergang = walk   *bummeln* = to stroll   *laufen* = to run OR to walk
   Laufclub = running club
10. *bieten* = to offer / provide   *anbieten* = to offer   *Angebot* = offer
11. *ungewöhnlich* = unusual   *fein* = fine / delicate   *mehrere* = several
12. *Landschaft* = countryside OR landscape   *Land* = country (*Länder* = countries)
13. *Grenze* = border / frontier
14. *Wanderweg* = footpath   *weg* = away   *unterwegs* = on the way
15. *Gebiet* = area / region   *Gegend* = landscape OR region
16. *Sehenswürdigkeiten* = sights / places of interest   *Aussicht* = view   *aussehen* = to look
    (*gut aussehen* = to look good)
17. *Burg* AND *Schloss* = castle
18. *Ort* = place   *irgendwo* = somewhere
19. *gespannt* = tense / strained OR eager
20. *tagsüber* = during the day   *Arbeitstag* = working day
21. *sich entspannen* = to relax   *entspannend* = relaxing   *sich ausruhen* = to rest
22. *ein gesunder Lebensstil* = healthy lifestyle   *gesund* = healthy   *Gesundheit* = health
    Essen = food   *Ernährung* = feeding OR diet   *Nahrungsmittel* = food(stuffs)
    Koch/Köchin = chef / cook   *kochen* = to cook
23. *Verhältnisse* = circumstances
24. *zuerst* = first / firstly   *erste/erster/erstes* = first BUT *erst* = only   *erste Hilfe* = First Aid
25. *übersehen* = to overlook / miss

8 Verbal Volley (VFLA)

The Verbal Volley is a fast-paced, fun, engaging and rapid-fire way to practise vocabulary which works in a similar way to the Blaster (VFLA #7), except that it is done in pairs. I use this VFLA to kick off practice and tell the students that it's a good way to warm up the language.

Students work in pairs as A and B. They look at the list of vocabulary on the board. Starting from the top of the list A says the Target Language words and English on the first line, followed by B saying the Target Language words and English on the second line. A and B alternate until they reach the bottom of the list. The first pair to do this bob up to show that they have won.

As with the Blaster VFLA, you need to get the class used to how this works and ensure that everyone is motivated to say their word: by not speaking the Target Language and the English they are letting their partner down. Of course, even though it's fast, intelligible language must be heard. While fun, it is still serious practice!

Once the class has been trained in Verbal Volley it is an invaluable VFLA for maximising practice with of a lot of vocabulary in a short amount of time.

As with the Blaster, it works well as a last-minute massed practice strategy, such as in the run-up to a GCSE reading or listening exam, followed by a pacy retrieval test of key vocabulary.

Testing retrieval after a couple of Verbal Volleys immediately shows students how much language knowledge they have picked up, so make sure they are aware of this. Have a mock celebratory Target Language cheer for the winning pair of students, then run the Verbal Volley again from the bottom of the list of projected vocabulary and ask the class if they think they can beat the pair who won last time.

Preparation and resources

- Identify the group of Target Language words or phrases that you want to practise with a class (there is an example on page 64 and many more available at www.crownhouse.co.uk/featured/fun-mfl). Copy the vocabulary or phrases onto a PowerPoint slide and number each item.
- Arrange your classroom seating plan so that you can divide the class into halves.
- Project the vocabulary or phrases onto the board so that every student can see them.

Instructions

- Tell the class they are going to do a Verbal Volley, but first you will model it for them. Ask for a student volunteer to work with you.
- With the volunteer, explain that you will take turns to say all of the Target Language words and the English for each numbered line on the projected list. You will read the first line, the student the second, and so on, until one of you has said the last item on the vocabulary list, at which point you both bob up.
- Model the Verbal Volley for a few turns. Stop modelling as soon as the students have understood.
- Tell the class to work with the student next to them and to decide who is Student A and Student B. A goes first, followed by B.
- This is a competition so everyone must say all the words and no skipping.
- Put a tally mark on the board for the side with the students who win the Verbal Volley.

Variations to the VFLA

- Vary the starting point: run one Verbal Volley from the top of the list and then shout out, 'Verbal Volley! From the bottom!' Shout this out in Target Language if the group are well trained.
- Start from the top, go down to the bottom, then go back up to the top again.
- Get one student in the pair to say the Target Language and the other student to say the English meaning of it.

- Get one student to say the Target Language word, and spell the word using the Target Language alphabet, followed by the other student saying the English meaning.
- Project an irregular verb table onto the board.
- Get the students to do the Verbal Volley in groups of three or four.
- Add some action! Each student has to bob up to say the Target Language vocab and English meaning, and sit down again, before the turn passes to the other student. (I tried this once as part of a cross-curricular MFL PE lesson with students doing a circuit routine where one student was doing a press-up or sit-up while the other student called out the Target Language word and English from a handout; then they swapped. This kind of thing certainly creates a buzz and gets students talking about language lessons.)

Teacher notes

Students must know *how* to pronounce the words correctly before running this VFLA.

Here's a vocab list in Spanish to get you started
(also available at www.crownhouse.co.uk/featured/fun–mfl)

1. *apoyar* = to support   *apoyo* = support
2. *mitad* = half   *a mitad de precio* = half-price
3. *bolsillo* = pocket   *dinero de bolsillo* = pocket money
4. *educado* = polite   *educadamente* = politely   *maleducado* = rude
5. *equipo* = team OR equipment   *deportes de equipo* = team sports
   trabajar en equipo = to work in a team
6. *perder* = to lose OR to miss (train, etc.)   (*pierde* = he / she loses OR misses)
   ganar = to win OR to earn   *ganarse la vida* = to earn a living
   estilo de vida = lifestyle
7. *echar de menos* = to miss (a person)
8. *conseguir* = to get / obtain   (*conseguir experiencia laboral* = to get work experience)
9. *pasar un buen rato/divertirse/pasarlo bien* = ALL TO DO WITH HAVING A
   GOOD TIME
10. *pasar un mal rato/pasarlo mal/fatal* = ALL TO DO WITH HAVING A BAD TIME
    un rato = a while
11. *marcharse* = to leave   *salir de* + noun = to leave (a place)
    (*salir de España* = to leave Spain)
12. *dejar de* + infinitive = to stop (doing something)
13. *solo* = alone BUT *sólo/solo* AND *solamente* = only / just *trabajar solo* = to work alone
14. *tener miedo* = to be scared   *miedo* = fear
15. *sequía* = drought   *grifo* = tap   *tener sed/hambre* = to be thirsty / hungry
16. *golpear* = to hit   *golpes* = blows / knocks
17. *creer* = to believe   *creencia* = belief
18. *ayudar* = to help   *ayuda* = help
19. *peor* – worse   *mejor* = better
20. *resultar* = to turn out to be   (*resultó genial* = it turned out to be great)
    (*resulta que* = it turns out that)
21. *sacar fotos* = to take photos
22. *emocionante* = exciting   *emocionarse* = to get excited   (*nos emocionó* = it thrilled us)
23. *robo* = robbery   *ladrón* = thief
24. *paraguas* = umbrella
25. *entender* AND *comprender* = to understand
26. *avisar* = to warn   ¡*ojo!* AND ¡*cuidado!* = watch out!   *aviso* = notice / warning
27. *bachillerato* = A levels
28. *recordar* = to remind OR to remember (*recuerdo* = I remind OR I remember)
    recuerdos = souvenirs   *acordarse* = to remember (*me acuerdo* = I remember)

9 Vhispers (VFLA)

Q: What do you get when you cross vocabulary and whispers?

A: Another way to practise vocabulary before testing retrieval.

Vhispers works as follows: with the class split into two, tell one student from each side to look at the projected list on the board. Tell the rest of the class to shut their eyes. Point to three Target Language words on the list, and the two students with their eyes open then whisper these words and English meanings to the students sitting next to them. They in turn whisper to the students next to them and so on until the Vhispers reach the last student in the line. This student now walks to the board to touch and speak what they believe to be the original whispered vocabulary. The student who does this first wins a point for their side.

If the whispered words are not identified correctly then the process is repeated until the whispered words are identified correctly.

Vhispers is competitive, and can be used effectively to slow down the pace a little after a few rapid-fire VFLAs.

Afterwards, take a moment to discuss with the students their favourite word and least favourite from the ones that have just been whispered before running Vhispers again, running another VFLA or testing retrieval.

Preparation and resources

- Identify the group of Target Language words or phrases that you want to practise with a class (there is an example on page 67 and many more at www.crownhouse.co.uk/featured/fun-mfl). Copy the vocabulary or phrases onto a PowerPoint slide. It is better NOT to number them this time (see the teacher notes below).
- Arrange your classroom seating plan so you can divide the class into halves.
- Project the vocabulary or phrases onto the board so that every student can see them.

Instructions

- Tell the class that this is a race with each side of the class competing against the other.
- Explain that you are going to choose three words from the projected list, but only the two students sitting closest to the board from each side of the class will see what the words are. They will be the Vhispers Leaders.
- Tell the class that you want everyone apart from the Vhispers Leaders to close their eyes.
- Put your finger on three different Target Language words on the board that you want the Vhispers Leaders to remember.
- When you say the Target Language word for 'go' the rest of the class open their eyes. The Vhispers Leaders whisper the three Target Language words and English to the student next to them.
- That student then whispers the three words to the *next* student along on their side, and so on, until the Vhispers reach the last student.
- The last student walks to the board, touches the three Target Language words and English and speaks them aloud.
- If they are correct, that side wins. If not, tell the class that the VFLA must start again.

Variations to the VFLA

- Start Vhispers with the student at the back on each side.
- Adopt a class vs. clock approach. Start the Vhispers off with just one student with their eyes open, who then whispers the words to the next student and so on to the last student who then identifies the whispered vocabulary. Stop the clock and make a note of the time, before running it again to see if the class can better the time.

Teacher notes

Insist on fair play. Students must whisper words, not the numbers. Make students aware that you know how they could cheat but that's not in the spirit of the VFLA. To avoid this, have your slides of vocabulary without numbers.

Have the same number of students on each side. Any extra student acts as a Vhispers Monitor to check that the other side is carrying out the VFLA fairly.

Here's a vocab list in French to get you started (also available at www.crownhouse.co.uk/featured/fun–mfl)

1. *blesser* = to injure   *blessure* – injury   *se faire mal* = to hurt oneself
2. *quinzaine* AND *quinze jours* = fortnight
3. *déchets/ordures* = rubbish
4. *au lieu de ...* = instead of ...
5. *auto* = car   *automobilistes* = drivers   *car/autocar* = coach
6. *essayer de* + infinitive = to try to ...   *période d'essai* = trial period
7. *en même temps* = at the same time
8. *moche/laid* = ugly
9. *perdre* = to lose   *perte de temps* = waste of time
10. *apprendre* = to learn   (*j'ai appris* = I learnt)
11. *bac* – A levels   *brevet des collèges* = GCSE
12. *j'en ai marre* = I've had enough
13. *grève* = strike
14. *journée* = day
15. *faire la grasse matinée* = to have a lie-in
16. *ménage* = housework
17. *faire les courses/faire les magasins/faire du shopping/faire des achats* = ALL TO DO WITH SHOPPING   *faire provision* = to stock up
18. *repas* = meal   *nourriture* = food   *nourrir* = to feed
19. *être en colère/être fâché contre/se fâcher contre* = ALL TO DO WITH BEING ANGRY
20. *ado/adolescent* = teenager
21. *soldes* = sales
22. *sacs à main* = handbags   *bagues* = rings   *boucles d'oreille* = earrings
23. *stage* = work experience placement
24. *vers* = around (with time)   *environ* = about (approximately)
25. *banc* = bench
26. *monde* = world   *tout le monde* = everybody   *du monde* = a lot of people

10 The Drama Game (VFLA)

I once observed a drama lesson where a colleague used an activity to get the class to count up to eleven. The teacher starts by saying 'one'. After that, anyone in the class (apart from the teacher) says 'two' and then someone says 'three' and so on until eleven is reached. Sound easy? There's a catch.

The rules are: if two or more people speak (and this includes even starting to speak) the same number at the same time then the activity has to restart with the teacher saying 'one' again. If a student says a number they are not allowed to say the consecutive number, so if a student says 'three' they cannot then say 'four'.

Some language teachers do this with Target Language numbers not only as a way of practising the numbers but also as a 'fun filler' in the last five minutes before the end of a lesson. I have also seen it done starting with the whole class standing; students who say the number at the same time must sit down to show that they are out.

I love the arbitrary nature of the activity and the tension created by the uncertainty of who might put their foot in it. When I was putting together the VFLAs, it got me thinking about how this could be used to practise words rather than numbers. Why couldn't I just apply the same activity to a list of words that I wanted the students to practise? I created a PowerPoint slide, projected this onto the board and explained that I would start by saying the Target Language and the English for the first word at the top of the projected list. After this, anyone in the group was free to say the Target Language and English for the second word down the list and so on right down to the last word at the bottom of the list.

Preparation and resources

- Identify the group of Target Language words or phrases you want to practise with a class (there is an example on page 71 and many more at www.crownhouse.co.uk/featured/fun-mfl). Copy the vocabulary or phrases onto a PowerPoint slide and number each item.
- Arrange your classroom seating plan so that you can divide the class into two.
- Project the vocabulary or phrases onto the board so that every student can see the language.

Instructions

- Tell the students that the aim of the whole class is to have reached and said the last word on the projected list.
- Explain that you will always start the activity by saying the Target Language word or phrase and the English meaning for number one on the projected PowerPoint slide.
- Once you have said the first word or phrase anyone else in the class is free to say the Target Language and the English meaning for the second item on the list.
- Point out that that student cannot then say the word or phrase immediately after this; a different student must say it. They are free to say another later but not *consecutive* words or phrases.
- This process continues with random students speaking out the words or phrases in the order they appear on the slide until two or more students start to say the word or phrase at the same time. When this happens the process must start again with you speaking the Target Language word or phrase and the English meaning for number one.
- Tell the class that everyone must be looking at the projected slide of vocabulary or phrases at all times.

Variations to the VFLA

- Start the activity from the last word or phrase on the projected slide and work your way up to the top.
- Try side versus side. It can get complicated in a big class and therefore works better with fewer students, but it's a good alternative from you directing the whole-class version.

You need to keep an eye and ear out for students on either side who say the words at the same time within their sides.

- Get the class to stand up initially. Individual students must sit down once they have said a Target Language word and English meaning.

Teacher notes

If some students are a lot more confident than others you may find that they dominate this VFLA. If so, run the last variation above: those who have spoken sit down. Once they have sat down give them an extension task so that they're not waiting passively for the VFLA to finish. Make sure that the whole class are aware of any potential extension tasks before running this VFLA.

Insist that every student is focused on the vocabulary on the projected list. They must be looking at the board and hearing what is said by other students, not watching to see whose lips are about to move!

Sometimes with a very enthusiastic group it can be a bit tricky to move on from the first two Target Language words as everyone wants to speak. If this is the case, vary where you start from in the list; talk to the class and calm the situation.

Here's a vocab list in German to get you started
(also available at www.crownhouse.co.uk/featured/fun-mfl)

1. *rote Ampel* = red (traffic) light   *Verkehr* = traffic
2. *Unfall* = accident
3. *schlank* = slim   *dick* = fat   *riesig* = huge
4. *wenig* = little
5. *Fleisch* = meat   *Gemüse* = vegetables   *Fett* = fat
6. *Sportarten* = sports   *Sportler/Sportlerin* = sportsman/sportswoman
   Sport treiben = to do sport   *Tennisverein* = tennis club   *Federball* = badminton
   Sportplatz = sports field   *Mitglied* = member
7. *Tanzgruppe* = dance group
8. *Flug* = flight   *Rückflug* = return flight
9. *-los* = without   (*problemlos* = without problems)   (*arbeitslos* = unemployed)
10. *wohnen* = to live OR to stay   *Hauptstadt* = capital city
11. *Kleider/Kleidung/Klamotten* = clothes   *einkaufen gehen* = to go shopping
12. *Preise* = prices   *teuer* = expensive   (*nicht*) *billig* = (not) cheap   *preiswert* = cheap
    günstig = at a reasonable price   *preisgünstig* = cheap   *mäßig* = moderate (price)
13. *Karten* = tickets (to a match, etc.) OR cards   *Fahrkarten* = tickets (for travel)
    Eintrittskarten = admission tickets
14. *so ein Pech!* = what bad luck!
15. *empfehlen* = to recommend
16. *Wellen* = waves
17. *vermieten* = to rent out/hire out/let   *mieten* = to rent/hire   *Miete* = rent
    Mietwagen = rental car/hire car
18. *früher* = previously/in the past
19. *Gleis* = platform OR track   *Abteil* = compartment
20. *Speisewagen* = dining car   *Speisekarte* = menu   *Vorspeise* = starter
    Hauptgericht = main course   *Nachspeise* AND *Nachtisch* = dessert
    Gerichte AND *Speisen* = dishes (food)
21. *gepflegt* = neat/trim/smart   *hilfsbereit* = helpful
22. *Anlage* = facility/establishment   *Personal* = staff   *vorhanden* = available
23. *vollkommen* = completely   *überrascht* = surprised
24. *Möglichkeiten* = possibilities   *unmöglich* = impossible
25. *sich erkundigen* = to enquire
26. *Fahrrad* = bike   *Rennrad* = racing bike

11 Group Bob–Up (VFLA)

After using Bob-Up Classic as a rapport-building exercise in which one student adopted the role of the teacher running the VFLA while I adopted the student role, I thought that if a student could run Bob-Up Classic at the front of the class, then there was no reason why students couldn't also take on the teacher role in a small group. Thus was born the concept of 'classrooms within a classroom'.

By sticking up MWBs around the room I could duplicate in each group what was happening on a larger scale with the whole class. I was creating mini-classroom spaces each with its own whiteboard. In terms of resources, this is a simple low-tech job: you just need some MWBs and some marker pens. Tom Bennett, in *Teacher Proof*,[10] reminds us that teaching doesn't have to have a lot of tech – and marker pens and boards avoid the problems you *sometimes* get with IT.

This works well with students in groups of three. In front of each MWB you place two chairs. Each group of three nominates a 'teacher-student', who stands at the MWB. The other students sit on the chairs facing the list of vocab on the board at the front.

The teacher-student in each group calls out a number for a word on the projected list and awards a point to whichever of the students bobs up first and calls out the Target Language and English.

---

[10] T. Bennett, (2013) *Teacher Proof: Why Research in Education Doesn't Always Mean What it Claims, and What You Can Do About it*, Abingdon, Routledge. pp. 132–133.

It sounds very similar to the Bob-Up Classic (VFLA #1), except that instead of you directing proceedings from the front, you now have mini-versions of this around the room – Bob-Up Classic replicas, if you like. All you need to say by means of explanation is, 'You know what we do with Bob-Up, well, you are going to do that in threes on the MWB. It's what we do as a class but in groups on the walls.'

While the students are running Bob-Up Classic on MWBs around the room you wander and monitor. After ten minutes or so you could test each group's retrieval of the vocabulary.

This got me thinking that many of the VFLAs could also be replicated this way. With groups running Bob-Up Classic at the MWBs, there are students bobbing up and down at random around the classroom. Suddenly you call out the name of another VFLA and the teacher-students in each group start running the new VFLA with their students. Then I might call out 'test retrieval!' and project the slide with the English meaning covered up and each group works together to write down the words they know the meaning of.

This is where things work better on the bigger MWBs than on mini-whiteboards.

This is *black-belt VFLA proficiency* which relies on students knowing all the VFLAs you use with a class. Once you have a well-trained class, they will be able to adapt and run any VFLA for themselves and it is heartening to see students taking the lead and adopting the role of the teacher. You might even want to leave it up to the teacher-students when to change VFLA instead of you prompting them.

Preparation and resources

- Identify the group of Target Language words or phrases that you want to practise with a class (there is an example on page 75 and many more at www.crownhouse. co.uk/featured/fun-mfl). Copy the vocabulary or phrases onto a PowerPoint slide and number each item.
- Stick up sufficient MWBs around your classroom for groups of three students to work at them.
- Arrange your classroom seating plan so that you can divide the class into halves. Place two chairs in front of each MWB all facing the board at the front.
- Project the vocabulary or phrases onto the board so that every student can see them.

Instructions

- Tell the class to get into groups of three and then to stand in front of one of the MWBs around the walls of the classroom.

- Give the class five seconds to decide who will be the teacher-student and who will be Student A and Student B.
- Tell A and B to sit down on the chairs facing the board at the front of the class. Give each teacher-student a marker pen. They stand behind A and B also facing the front.
- Explain that the teacher-student is going to run their own Bob-Up Classic VFLA on their MWB, and keep score.
- The teacher-student runs their Group Bob-Up in the same way you run Bob-Up Classic as the class teacher: they call out a number from the list and the first student, A or B, to bob up and call out the Target Language and English for that number wins the point for themselves.
- The teacher-student tallies the score on the MWB.

Variations to the VFLA

- The variations for the Group Bob-Up VFLA are actually other VFLAs. The teacher-student could move on to Señor Hunton Dice (VFLA #15), then two or three minutes later they could change to Random Random (VFLA #3). Then the same variations *within* each VFLA exist as options to the teacher-students.
- Vary the group size; have groups of five with one student as teacher at the MWBs.

Teacher notes

It takes a trained class to do the Group Bob-Up VFLA, mainly because students need to know how Bob-Up Classic works first. However, once the students are *au fait* with Bob-Up Classic they will know how to replicate this in their groups of three.

Having the whole class working in small groups gets the students practising more vocabulary than they would be doing as a side versus side activity with you directing proceedings.

**Here's a vocab list in Spanish to get you started
(also available at www.crownhouse.co.uk/featured/fun-mfl)**

1. *hacer una llamada* = to make a call   *llamar* = to call
2. *tecla* = key (computer)
3. *recoger* = to pick up   (*recoger basura* = to pick up rubbish)
4. *reírse de* = to laugh about
5. *descubrir* = to discover
6. *caer* = to fall
7. *flor* = flower
8. *siglo* = century
9. *tienda* = shop OR tent
10. *organización benéfica* = charity   *fines benéficos* = charitable causes
11. *pobreza* = poverty   *pobre* = poor   *rico* = rich
12. *tirar* = to throw away   *basura* = rubbish
13. *tener suerte* = to be lucky
14. *gente* = people
15. *reutilizar* = to reuse
16. *clientes* = customers
17. *concurso* = competition
18. *humos tóxicos* = toxic smoke
19. *campo* = countryside   *paisaje* = landscape
20. *envases de cristal* = glass containers
21. *albergue juvenil* = youth hostel
22. *descuento* = discount
23. *rebajas* = sales
24. *senderismo* = hiking
25. *canguro* = babysitter
26. *despejado* = clear / cloudless (sky)

12 Vlotto (VFLA)

This VFLA came about because I wanted to adapt the traditional way of playing bingo with numbers to using lists of vocabulary, similar to Paul Ginnis's Academic Bingo.[11] This blend of vocab and lotto I call Vlotto.

My first attempt involved projecting a vocabulary list onto the board, such as the example on page 79. I asked the students to identify six Target Language words that they would not know the meaning of if they saw them on a reading paper or heard them on a listening paper, and then write them down together with their English meaning. These were the words I wanted the students to practise.

Once the students had chosen their six words I would arbitrarily call out Target Language words from the list on the board and put a tick next to the words on the board so the students could see which words had been said.

Whichever Target Language word I called out, I wanted the whole class to shout out the English, irrespective of whether that was one of their six words. Whenever I called out a word that a student had written down as one of their six words, they put a tick next to that word.

---

11 P. Ginnis, (2002) *The Teacher's Toolkit: Raise Classroom Achievement with Strategies for Every Learner*, Carmarthen, Crown House Publishing. p. 73.

The winner, as in bingo, was the student who had all six of their words ticked off first. I got the winner to call out the Target Language for each word they had ticked off, and the rest of the class called out the English meaning. I also awarded a point to the side to which the winning student belonged.

I have since adapted this VFLA by asking the students to choose six Target Language words and their meanings and then to rate the words from one to six according to how much they like each one. Willingham sums this up: '… if you give people a simple task in which they *must* think of the meaning – for example, rating how much they like each word – they will remember the words quite well.'[12]

Preparation and resources

- Identify the group of Target Language words or phrases that you want to practise with a class (there is an example on page 79 and many more at www.crownhouse. co.uk/featured/fun-mfl). Copy the vocabulary or phrases onto a PowerPoint slide and number each item.
- Arrange your classroom seating plan so you can divide the class into halves.
- Project the vocabulary slide onto the board so that every student can see it.

Instructions

- Tell the class to choose and write down six Target Language words and their meaning from the projected list of key vocabulary. They must be words that they would not know the meaning of if they were to read them in a text or hear them spoken.
- Tell the class that you are going to read out the Target Language words from the list at random and that each time you call out a word you will put a tick next to it.
- Every time you read out a Target Language word they must call out the English for it. If it is one of the six words they have chosen, they put a tick next to it.
- The VFLA continues until a student has ticked off their six words. The student then bobs up and calls out 'Vlotto' to be crowned Vlotto Winner.

Variations to the VFLA

- Just read the English meaning and all the students shout out the Target Language for it.
- Project a verb table onto the board instead of key vocabulary.

---

12 Willingham, (2009) p. 83.

- Vary the number of words you ask students to write down.
- Students work in groups of three. The teacher-student calls out Target Language words from the projected slide on the board and the other two students call out the English for it. To make this more efficient, the teacher-student either notes down the numbers for the Target Language words or they have a handout of the list and they tick the words on that.

Teacher notes

I use Vlotto as the first of six or so different VFLAs before testing retrieval, usually at the start of the lesson. In many ways it works as what the TEEP initiative would refer to as a 'bell work' activity: an activity right at the start of the lesson to help students focus on immediately starting a task.[13]

What matters is how the students are encouraged to select the words. If they think about their six Vlotto words by ranking them, there is more chance of these words sticking.

---

[13] See http://www.teep.org.uk/news.asp.

Here's a vocab list in French to get you started
(also available at www.crownhouse.co.uk/featured/fun–mfl)

1. *printemps* = spring   *été* = summer   *automne* = autumn   *hiver* = winter
2. *embouteillage* AND *bouchon* = traffic jam
3. *route* = road
4. *se coucher* = to go to bed
5. *portable* = mobile phone   *ascenseur* = lift
6. *faire de l'équitation/faire du cheval/monter à cheval* = ALL TO DO WITH HORSE-RIDING
7. *faire du vélo/faire du cyclisme/faire des balades à vélo* = ALL TO DO WITH CYCLING
    faire du VTT = to go mountain-biking
8. *usine* = factory   *ouvrier* = worker
9. *faire la vaisselle* = to do the washing-up   *passer l'aspirateur* = to do the vacuuming
10. *agaçant* = irritating   *agacer/embêter/énerver* = to annoy   *méchant* = nasty
11. *gratuit* = free (of charge)   *accès gratuit* = free access/entry
    appels gratuits = free calls
12. *libre* = free (not occupied)   *occupé* = taken (seat, taxi, etc.)
13. *cher* = expensive
14. *bon marché* AND *pas cher* = cheap
15. *facteur* = postman   *factrice* = postwoman
16. *métier* = profession/job
17. *demeurer* = to live (somewhere)
18. *démarrer/débuter/commencer* = to start
19. *notes* = marks   (*bonnes/mauvaises notes* = good/bad marks)
20. *prêter de l'argent* = to lend some money
21. *commerce* = business
22. *chanteur/chanteuse* = singer   *chanson* = song
23. *il y a* + time phrase = ago   (*il y a deux ans* = two years ago)
24. *infirmier/infirmière* = nurse
25. *balcon* = balcony   (*chambre avec balcon* = room with a balcony)
    donner sur = to look out over (view)

13 Penalty Shoot-Out (VFLA)

When I came up with this VFLA I felt like I was really getting into my stride with designing them. This is an activity that I thought would work especially well with boys. As Amanda Barton says in the section on motivating boys in *Getting the Buggers Into Languages*: 'For some boys, and girls, games are the only redeeming feature of language lessons.'[14]

The Penalty Shoot-Out VFLA is also based on students being exposed to a lot of vocabulary on a projected slide, but it is not as rapid fire as other VFLAs. This is because the students in one team look at the vocabulary list on the board and choose the words that they believe will be the most difficult to translate correctly for the opposing team (who have their backs to the board). The side looking at the list can only shout out one word or phrase (normally *only* in the Target Language) to the other side. If that side, with their backs to the board, do not call out the correct translation then the first side call out the meaning – and have scored their penalty. If the side with their backs to the board guess the word correctly then they have saved the penalty.

This VFLA works as a way of creating word discussion. In *The Vocabulary Book*, Michael F. Graves, writes:

> *Discussion is one method of actively processing word meanings, giving students the opportunity to hear and use the word in a variety of contexts and enabling students to learn from each other.*[15]

---

[14] Amanda Barton, (2006) *Getting the Buggers Into Languages*, London, Bloomsbury Education. p. 52.

[15] Michael F. Graves, (2005) *The Vocabulary Book: Learning & Instruction*, New York, Teachers College Press. p. 70.

In this context, the students discuss which words they think their classmates would struggle with knowing the meaning of and *why*.

Preparation and resources

- Identify the group of Target Language words or phrases that you want to practise with a class (there is an example on page 83 and many more at www.crownhouse. co.uk/featured/fun-mfl). Copy the vocabulary or phrases onto a PowerPoint slide and number each item.
- Arrange your classroom seating plan so that you can divide the class into Side A and Side B.
- Project the vocabulary or phrases onto the board.
- Write on a whiteboard near to the projected vocabulary the following:

	Side A	**Side B**
1:		
2:		
3:		
4:		
5:		
Total:		

Instructions

- Tell the students that one half of the class (Side B) will turn their backs to the board and the other half (Side A) will remain facing the board, looking at the projected vocabulary or phrases.
- Explain that the sides will take turns in doing this.
- The students facing the board have ten seconds to choose a Target Language (and only the Target Language) word that they believe will be difficult for the opposing team to translate correctly. They will then call out this word to the other side.
- Any student on Side B shouts out a translation. This is the *only* translation that you will accept. If Side B's translation is correct then Side B have saved Side A's first penalty; if it is incorrect then Side A have scored their first penalty.

- Put a tick or a cross on the whiteboard according to whether the side taking the penalty (calling the word out) scores the penalty or has the penalty saved. For example, put a tick underneath Side A to show that they have called a word out that Side B guessed incorrectly.

	Side A	Side B
1:	✔	
2:		
3:		
4:		
5:		
Total:		

- Side A then turn their backs to the board and Side B have ten seconds to discuss and choose a Target Language word and call it out to Side A. If Side A guess correctly then you put a cross under Side B.
- At the end of the five rounds the side which has scored the most penalties wins the VFLA.

Variations to the VFLA

- Allow students more than one 'save' (that is, more than one chance at guessing the translation).
- Conduct the VFLA with students in pairs or in groups of four with pairs against pairs as opposed to sides against sides.
- To make the VFLA more rapid fire reduce the amount of thinking time for students choosing the word or phrase.

Teacher notes

When students are looking at the projected slide on the board, they are identifying which words and phrases they think their classmates would and would not know. They are projecting their own abilities at retrieval onto other students in their class, reflecting on whether they would know the words themselves. This VFLA moves the focus away from cognates as students know that they will be highly unlikely to score a penalty calling out *le garage* for instance.

Also, with this VFLA there is more of an emphasis on hearing the word rather than seeing it.

Here's a vocab list in German to get you started (also available at www.crownhouse.co.uk/featured/fun-mfl)

1. *Ausflug* = trip   *Reise* = journey/trip   *Fahrt* = journey
   Weltreise = trip around the world   *besichtigen* AND *besuchen* = to visit
   Besuch = visit   *Besichtigung* = tour   *Schifffahrt* = shipping
2. *reisen* = to travel   *Reisefirma* = tour agency   *Reisebüro* = travel agency
3. *Ankunft* = arrival   *Abfahrt* − departure   *Aufenthalt* = stay
4. *Bauernhof* = farm   *Landwirt* = farmer
5. *Leute* AND *Menschen* = people   *Jugendliche* = young people
6. *wieder hinfahren* = to go back again
7. *Besitzer* = owner
8. *Strand* = beach   *an der Küste* = on the coast   *das Meer* AND *die See* = the sea
   BUT *der See* = the lake   *Sonnenschirm* = sunshade/umbrella/parasol
   Regenschirm = umbrella
9. *Bad* = bath   *Dusche* = shower
10. *loben* = to praise
11. *(un)abhängig* = (in)dependent
12. *aufwachsen* = to grow up
13. *Kühe* = cows
14. *gute/schlechte Noten bekommen* = to get good/bad marks   *Schulnoten* = marks
    verbessern = to improve
15. *Arzt* = doctor   *Notarzt* = emergency doctor   *Tierarzt* = vet
16. *faul* = lazy   *herumsitzen* = to sit around
17. *frech* = cheeky
18. *Klassenfahrt* = school trip   *Heimfahrt* = journey home
19. *anfangen* = to start   *Anfänger* = beginner(s)
20. *beide* = both
21. *Schlagzeuger* = drummer
22. *üben* = to practise   *aufnehmen* = to record (CD, etc.)
23. *gewissenhaft* = conscientious
24. *Erfolg* = success   *erfolgreich* = successful
25. *plötzlich* = suddenly

14 Mr Writer (VFLA)

Let me clarify that Mr Writer doesn't have to be *Mr* Writer; it can also be Miss Writer, Ms Writer or Mrs Writer.

This VFLA is about copying. The students copy the words and phrases from the projected slide into their exercise books. However, this is what I would call 'goal-orientated copying' as the goal is to get to the bottom of the list of vocabulary or phrases first. Again, it involves competition and requires that you maintain the pace with the students. The sense of competition is important because you want to motivate students to copy vocabulary. However, there is a little more to it than that.

Researchers Anne Mangen, of the University of Stavanger in Norway, and Jean-Luc Velay state the following:

> *Writing by hand is fundamentally different from typing on a computer. And people who are learning new letters – such as children learning to read for the first time, or as adults picking up a second language with new characters – retain the information best when writing the letters by hand.*[16]

They found that according to the study:

---

[16] Anne Mangen and Jean-Luc Velay, (2010) 'Digitizing Literacy: Reflections on the Haptics of Writing', in Mehrdad Hosseini Zadeh (Ed.) *Advances in Haptics*, InTech, DOI: 10.5772/8710. Available from: http://www.intechopen.com/books/advances-in-haptics/digitizing-literacy-reflections-on-the-haptics-of-writing.

The physical act of holding a pencil and shaping letters sends feedback signals to the brain. This leaves a 'motor memory', which later makes it easier to recall the information connected with the movement.[17]

Students work in pairs. Student A copies the first line of Target Language and English from the slide on the board into a shared exercise book, speaks the Target Language and the English and then passes the book to B who then writes down the second line and speaks what they have just written.

Students' handwriting can get a little messy, so as the teacher insist that their handwriting has to be *legible* to the *teacher*. If it isn't, they have to start from scratch and risk not winning a point for their team. (I have also tried this where several of the English meanings have letters missing, so that students are also having to think more about the meaning of what they are copying.)

Many of the VFLAs create a noisy, exciting, competitive, engaging and ultimately knowledge-rich classroom – none more so than Mr/Mrs/Ms/Miss Writer.

Preparation and resources

- Identify the group of Target Language words or phrases that you want to practise with a class (there is an example on page 87 and many more available at www.crownhouse.co.uk/featured/fun-mfl). Copy the vocabulary or phrases onto a PowerPoint slide and number each item.
- Arrange your classroom seating plan so you can divide the class into two.
- Project the vocabulary or phrases onto the board so that every student can see them.

Instructions

- Tell students they will be working in pairs as Student A and Student B.
- Each pair has one exercise book between them.
- Say that you will do a countdown in the Target Language. Student A copies down the first Target Language word (or phrase) and the English meaning from the PowerPoint slide on the board.
- A then speaks the Target Language and English before handing the book to B who does the same (writing and speaking) with the second Target Language word or phrase on the list.

---

[17] Mangen and Velay, (2010).

- The first pair to reach the bottom of the list have to bob up with their exercise book for the teacher to check that their written list is *legible*. If it is legible they win; if not the VFLA continues until a pair bob up with a *legible* list.

Variations to the VFLA

- Student A could copy the Target Language word or phrase and say this, and then B could copy the English meaning and say it.
- Start the activity at different points in the list.
- Run the VFLA in groups of three or four.
- Instead of copying into an exercise book, give each pair of students a marker pen and conduct the VFLA on MWBs around the room. Seeing pairs of students on the various MWBs copying words and speaking them, then handing the pen to their partner makes for an incredibly liberated classroom, freed from the shackles of the usual seating plan!

Teacher notes

The element of competition has to be in place with this VFLA. It is copying, fast copying with a goal and a dash of thinking.

At some point get the students to think of the meaning of what they have copied. You could do this after the winning pair have been identified. Get the rest of the class to stop and get everyone to note their five most difficult words to write and why, the five easiest to write, their favourite words to write and why, and so on.

**Here's a vocab list in Spanish to get you started
(also available at www.crownhouse.co.uk/featured/fun-mfl)**

1. *billete de ida y vuelta* = return ticket
2. *abuelo* = grandfather   *abuela* = grandmother   *abuelos* = grandparents
3. *nacer* = to be born   *nacimiento* = birth   *fecha de nacimiento* = date of birth
   lugar de nacimiento = place of birth   *pueblo de nacimiento* = town of birth
4. *mostrar* = to show
5. *controlar el ratón* = to control the mouse (computer)
6. *regalar* = to give / present (as a gift)   *regalo* = present
7. *éxito* = success   *exitoso* = successful   *tener éxito* = to be successful
   lograr = to get / achieve
8. *gastar* = to spend   *malgastar* = to waste
9. *moda* = fashion   *estar a la moda* = to be in fashion   *ropa de moda* = fashionable clothes
10. *entenderse bien con* AND *llevarse bien con* = to get on well with
11. *mudarse de casa* = to move house
12. *acabar de* + infinitive = to have just (done something)
13. *mandar/enviar correos (electrónicos)* = to send emails
    mandar mensajes = to send messages / texts
14. *estar harto de* = to be sick of   (*estoy harto/a de ser camarero/a* = I'm sick of being a
    waiter / waitress)
15. *sobresaliente* = outstanding   *sacar sobresaliente* = to do brilliantly / get brilliant marks /
    get 'straight As'
16. *reglas* = rules
17. *cumplir* = to have a birthday   (*¿cuándo cumples?* = when is your birthday?)
    (*cumplir 16 años* = to celebrate one's 16th birthday)
18. *sacar buenas notas* = to get good marks
19. *enfadarse* = to get angry   *enfadado* = angry
20. *hacer los deberes* = to do homework
21. *gritar* = to shout
22. *cantidad* = quantity BUT *calidad* = quality
23. *tomar el sol* = to sunbathe
24. *diseñar* = to design
25. *celebrarse* AND *tener lugar* = to take place
26. *ahorrar* = to save (money)   *ahorro* = saving   (*ahorro de gasolina* = petrol saving)
27. *hijo* = son   *hija* = daughter   *hijos* = children   *nietos* = grandchildren
28. *entrevista* = interview

15 Señor Hunton Dice (VFLA)

This is my favourite VFLA, and not just because my name's on it. (I did think about removing my name, but the title of the VFLA became iconic with one class so I have left it. However, the students eventually dropped the *Señor Hunton* bit and just referred to it as *Dice*, thus ending my bid for posterity …) Feel free to change the title to whatever language you want: *M. Hunton Dit*, *Herr Hunton Sagt* – and use your own name. Simon found that *Simon Says* worked well for him.

The concept behind this VFLA is simple. It's *Simon Says* with a big vocabulary list. Project a numbered vocabulary list on the board, as with other VFLAs, and assign each student a number which matches one of the items on the list – just like Bob-Up Classic (VFLA #1).

The teacher stands next to the list and calls out the numbers at random. However, there is a twist … students should only stand up and call out their Target Language word and English *if* the teacher has also said a Target Language cue-word. Choose your own cue-word: '¡*Vaya!*', '*Allez!*' and '*Jetzt!*' do the job, but any word will do, perhaps one that the students have found particularly difficult to remember. If you say a number without saying the cue-word after and then a student bobs up and says their assigned word then take a point off that side's score (which could mean sometimes going into the red). You could be mean and say that even if a student so much as *twitches* when you have not said the cue-word, you still take a point off their team.

I could have included this VFLA in the variation section of Bob-Up Classic but I think that it merits inclusion as a VFLA in its own right.

Preparation and resources

- Identify the group of Target Language words or phrases that you want to practise with a class (there is an example on page 90 and many more at www.crownhouse. co.uk/featured/fun-mfl). Copy the vocabulary or phrases onto a PowerPoint slide and number each item.
- Arrange your classroom seating plan so that you can divide the class into halves.
- Project the vocabulary or phrases onto the board so that every student can see them.

Instructions (following Bob–Up Classic VFLA very closely)

- Ask for or choose two student captains to represent their side. Give them a captain's armband each.
- The captains have thirty seconds to give out all of the numbers for the words on the slide to all the students in their team.
- Once the students have their numbers they write down the word or words that are projected on the board.
- If there are more numbers on the slide than there are students on each side then some students will have to have more than one number (and therefore more than one word).
- Stand at the front of the class with the students facing the board with the vocabulary list projected and explain that you will call out any number (in English or the Target Language) for any of the words or phrases that the students are looking at.
- Explain that the students are only allowed to bob up and call out both the Target Language and the English phrase corresponding to the number that you call out *after* you have said a Target Language cue-word. Tell the students the cue-word.
- Explain that if you call a number out without the cue-word and a student bobs up or moves slightly then you will take a point off their team's total.
- Tally the marks for the winning team.
- Quickly call out another number for any of the other vocabulary or phrases and repeat the process.

Variations to the VFLA

The same variations exist for Señor Hunton Dice as they do for Bob-Up Classic. Here are a few more:

- Get students to swap numbers with the student sat next to them.
- Pull a quick switch between Bob-Up Classic and Señor Hunton Dice.
- Try *not* assigning numbers to students, so that as the class looks at the projected vocabulary list and you call out a number followed by your cue-word, it is the first student in the class to bob up and call out the Target Language and English to match

that number. This can get a little bit frenetic and in a big class it is sometimes difficult to see which student bobs up first!

Teacher notes

Señor Hunton Dice can be another rapid-fire VFLA. Calling out a number to match a word on the projected list, not saying the cue-word, calling out another number from the list and then saying the cue-word are all good rapport-building techniques with this VFLA.

Here's a vocab list in French to get you started (also available at www.crownhouse.co.uk/featured/fun-mfl)

1. *le lendemain* = the day after
2. *économiser* = to save
3. *informatique* = IT
4. *vedette* = star (celebrity)
5. *grand écran* = big screen (cinema)   *petit écran* = small screen (TV)
6. *accro* = addicted
7. *boum* = party
8. *personne ne ...* = nobody ...
9. *dépenser* = to spend (money)
10. *passer un examen* = to take an exam   *réussir à un examen* = to pass an exam
11. *cadet(te)* = younger   *aîné(e)* = elder
12. *camion* = lorry
13. *pièce* = room (of a house) OR play
14. *camarades/ami(e)s/copains/copines* = friends
15. *journal* = newspaper
16. *oublier* = to forget
17. *conseiller* = to advise   *conseil* = a piece of advice
18. *lire/faire de la lecture* = to read   *lecteur/lectrice* = reader
19. *dur* = hard
20. *je suis passionné(e) pour* = I'm fascinated / excited by
21. *il n'y a/avait pas assez de* = there aren't / weren't enough
22. *premiers secours* = first aid   *au secours!* = help!
23. *écouteurs* AND *casques* = headphones
24. *nouvelles/actualités/informations/infos* = news
25. *lieu* (plural *lieux*) AND *endroit* = place
26. *bouteilles vides* = empty bottles   *espace verte* = green space
27. *sucreries* AND *bonbons* = sweets

16 Mimey Mimey (VFLA)

Teaching words should be enjoyable. Pantomiming a verb such as dawdled should entertain.

Steven A. Stahl[18]

I couldn't agree more. Project the list of vocabulary, choose one of the words on the list without telling the students which it is, and keep miming the word until a student bobs up and calls out the correct Target Language and English. You have probably done mimes with nouns and verbs in the classroom before, and had students miming in pairs. The Mimey Mimey VFLA is designed to add a little light-heartedness to practising an awful lot of key vocabulary ahead of testing retrieval.

This VFLA is still rapid-fire-*ish*: it really depends on your ability and enthusiasm to keep on miming the words.

Preparation and resources

- Identify the group of Target Language words or phrases that you want to practise with a class (there is an example on page 93 and many more at www.crownhouse. co.uk/featured/fun-mfl). Copy the vocabulary or phrases onto a PowerPoint slide and number each item (although not essential for this VFLA).

---

[18] S. A. Stahl (1999), *Vocabulary Development*. Brookline, MA, Brookline Books. p. 52.

- Arrange your classroom seating plan so that you can divide the class into halves.
- Project the vocabulary or phrases onto the board so that every student can see them.

Instructions

- Tell the class that you are going to mime the meaning of one of the Target Language words on the projected vocabulary list in front of them.
- The first student to bob up and call out the Target Language and English for the word that you are miming wins the point for their team.
- You keep miming the word or phrase until a student bobs up and guesses the correct meaning.
- The students are free to bob up whenever they like (although exercise caution; if students are constantly bobbing up then set a compulsory thinking time of five seconds between bobbing up and guessing incorrectly and guessing again).
- Award a point to the team with the student who guesses correctly on it. Perform another mime with a different word.

Variations to the VFLA

- Instead of bobbing up, give each student a mini-whiteboard. Set a time limit on your mime. Have each student write and then reveal on their mini-whiteboards the Target Language and English for the word they thought you were miming.
- The students work in pairs at MWBs on the walls around the room. You mime a word and then see which pair can correctly guess it and write it up before the other pairs.

Teacher notes

The fiddly nature of organising pens and leaving mini-whiteboards on desks might interrupt the transition of moving from Mimey Mimey to another VFLA, but there's a possible solution to that in the teacher notes for Heads Down Thumbs Up to Vocab (VFLA #18).

Find some time to get students to think about the word meanings that you are miming. Before launching another mime discuss which words would be tricky to mime and why.

It's a great VFLA for building rapport with a class. A class watching you perform the same mime over and over is possibly not how you pictured teaching would be on your PGCE but it's a great way to show your human side! Getting students to do the same mime over and over also adds to the rapport for the same reason; you get to see everyone practising in a more relaxed way.

In *Classroom Instruction from A to Z*, Barbara Blackburn refers to needing to play with words in fun ways to help learning.[19] There aren't many more fun ways that combine light-hearted play with words and an exam-focused exposure of key vocabulary than Mimey Mimey.

Here's a vocab list in German to get you started (also available at www.crownhouse.co.uk/featured/fun–mfl)

1. *wahrscheinlich* = probably / likely
2. *zurückziehen* = to withdraw
3. *Bundeswehr* = (German) army
4. *eigen* = own   (*mein eigenes Restaurant* = my own restaurant)
5. *Volksmuseum* = national museum
6. *beschließen* = to decide
7. *Ausbildung* = training OR education
8. *Auto* AND *Wagen* = car
9. *Verkehrsamt* = tourist information office
10. *die Arbeit gefällt mir* = I enjoy the work
11. *Flugzeug* = plane
12. *teilen* = to share   (*ich teile ein Zimmer* = I share a room)
     teilnehmen = to take part   *mitmachen* = to take part / join in
13. *müde* = tired   *ermüdend* = tiring   *kaputt* = broken OR shattered (tired)
     erschöpft = exhausted   *anstrengend* = exhausting
14. *verstehen* = to understand   *verdienen* = to earn
15. *lustig* = funny   *fließend* = fluent
16. *Gebäude* = building
17. *Geschäftsmann/Geschäftsfrau* = businessman / businesswoman
18. *fühlen* = to feel
19. *Angst haben* = to be afraid   *fürchten* = to fear / be afraid of
20. *sitzen bleiben* = to repeat a year (at school)   *heiraten* = to marry
21. *allein* = alone
22. *lösen* = to solve   *Lösung* = solution
23. *werden* = to become
24. *manchmal* = sometimes
25. *Mahlzeiten* = meal times
26. *Rechtsanwalt* = lawyer

---

[19] Barbara Blackburn, (2007) *Classroom Instruction from A to Z*, Abingdon, Routledge. p. 129.

17 Spellingy Spellingy (VFLA)

Spellingy Spellingy was inspired by a teacher I saw in my NQT year. She handed out a list of French words and their English translations to the students and asked them to read the list of words. The students then looked up at the whiteboard as she started to write *letters* from one of the French words on the list. These letters were in any order, beginning, middle or end. As soon as students thought they knew which word the teacher was writing, they would call out the French word and the English meaning. The first to call out the correct word won the point for their team. If no one called out the correct word before the teacher had finished writing, the teacher began again with a different word.

I thought I could adapt this activity for a class using mini-whiteboards or in pairs using MWBs on the walls, so I made a few tweaks to turn it into a VFLA. Firstly, I wanted far more words projected. Secondly, I wanted to avoid students having to keep shifting focus from looking down at the handout to looking at the board at the front in order to check the spellings. Thirdly, it was easier to tell who had won by having students bobbing up rather than calling out the word. Fourthly, I decided to *mime* writing a Target Language word projected on the board. Having chosen a word I would use my marker pen with the cap still on and pretend to write this word continually until a student bobbed up and called out the correct Target Language and English for that word. I would repeat miming until someone got it. Because the students are focusing on the words projected in front of them, and hearing other students in the class calling out words from the list, they are constantly reminded of the Target Language and the meanings. Maybe it was me being picky but I preferred the students to focus on miming the spelling of the whole word, rather than drawing their attention to its constituent letters.

Finally, after a side has won a point on Spellingy Spellingy, I ask students which words they think would be the most difficult to spell, what their favourite words are, and to give me a quick rating of the last three words I had 'spelled'.

Preparation and resources

- Identify the group of Target Language words or phrases that you want to practise with a class (there is an example on page 96 and many more at www.crownhouse. co.uk/featured/fun-mfl). Copy the vocabulary or phrases onto a PowerPoint slide and number each item.
- Arrange your classroom seating plan so that you can divide the class into halves.
- Project the vocabulary or phrases onto the board so that every student can see them.

Instructions

- Tell the class that you are going to mime writing one of the Target Language words from the list of vocabulary projected on the board.
- Leave the cap on your marker pen and keep miming the spelling of the Target Language word until a student in the class bobs up and calls out the Target Language and English correctly.
- Students are free to bob up at any time and call out the Target Language and English, but you will only stop and award a point to the side when a student guesses correctly. Then you will repeat the process with a different Target Language word.

Variations to the VFLA

- As with the Group Bob-Up (VFLA #11) you could have students in groups of three at a MWB with one student being the teacher-student and the other two students *facing* them. The teacher-student chooses a Target Language word from the projected list at the front, and then mimes the spelling of that word on their MWB.

Teacher notes

It takes a certain level of focus for the teacher not to be put off their miming with students bobbing up and calling out the Target Language and English!

In between miming the spellings of words, ask students to think about which words are more difficult to spell in their view. Before switching to another VFLA or before practising retrieval, get the students to rate the top five Target Language words that they think would be the most difficult to spell.

Here's a vocab list in Spanish to get you started (also available at www.crownhouse.co.uk/featured/fun-mfl)

1. *según* = according to
2. *periódicos* = newspapers   *periodista* = journalist
3. *romper* = to break
   romperse el brazo / la pierna / el tobillo = to break one's arm / leg / ankle
   me he roto … = I have broken …   *roto* = broken
4. *sacar un título* = to get a degree   *sacar buenas/malas notas* = to get good / bad marks
5. *costar* = to cost   *cuesta demasiado* = it costs too much
6. *abrir los correos (electrónicos)* = to open emails
7. *hacer las compras* AND *ir de compras* = to go shopping / do the shopping
8. *contraseña* = password
9. *pasar* = to spend (time) BUT *gastar* = to spend (money)
10. *ponerse maquillaje* = to put on make-up   *vestirse* = to get dressed
    bien vestida = well dressed
11. *llegar a tiempo* = to arrive on time
12. *solicitar un empleo* = to apply for a job   *buscar trabajo* = to look for work
    carta de solicitud = letter of application
    (*escribir una carta de solicitud* = to write an application letter)
13. *empresa* = company
14. *taller* = workshop
15. *acoso* = bullying / harassment   *acoso escolar* = bullying in school
16. *cuenta* = bank account OR bill
17. *inconveniente* AND *desventaja* = disadvantage   *ventaja* = advantage
18. *nada* = nothing   *nunca* = never
19. *precioso* = beautiful
20. *hoy* = today   *hoy en día* = nowadays   *actualmente* = nowadays OR currently
    (ALL USED WITH PRESENT TENSE)
21. *falta de* = lack of
22. *al fondo de* = at the bottom of
23. *disfrutar de/gozar de/aprovechar* = to enjoy
24. *a menudo* = often
25. *aguantar* AND *soportar* = to put up with / bear

18 Heads Down Thumbs Up to Vocab (VFLA)

I can just about remember playing Heads Down Thumbs Up at primary school and in the first year at secondary school. It struck me as a fun way to use flashcards. It always followed the same pattern: the teacher chose four students, gave each a flashcard relating to a vocabulary item that we had been learning and had them stand at the front of the class holding their flashcards up so that the rest of the class could see both the student and the flashcard.

The teacher checked that we all knew the Target Language words on the flashcards by having the class call out each flashcard word. Next, the seated students put their heads down on the desk and their thumbs in the air. The four flashcard students went around and gently tweaked the thumbs of any four students at random before returning to the front and holding their flashcards up again. The four students who had had their thumbs tweaked would then stand up and guess who had tweaked them by calling out one of the flashcard words in the Target Language. Any student who guessed correctly swapped places with the student at the front for the next round.

I wondered if it was efficient enough for getting students to practise as much vocabulary as possible. The students who stood up and guessed only said one word, and there was no list projected on the board. I wanted to adapt this activity to include the vocabulary flooding that I referred to in Chapter 3. Focusing on just four flashcards was limiting; I wanted more words shown, more words spoken, and more words practised. So, I included more vocabulary: I projected the list on the board. I gave each student a piece of paper (or a mini-whiteboard) and asked them to write six key Target Language words and the English from the projected list in big handwriting. I also asked them to rate each word one to six as with Vlotto (VFLA #12).

I chose four students to bring their paper (or mini-whiteboards) to the front of the class, where they showed their list and spoke the words and their meaning with the rest of the class watching. In this way, instead of students speaking the single word on the flashcard, the Heads Down Thumbs Up To Vocab VFLA got more vocabulary practised in a shorter amount of time.

It also works as a side versus side competition, with three students from each side of the class tweaking the thumbs of students on the opposing side. This version is described below.

Preparation and resources

- Identify the group of Target Language words or phrases that you want to practise with a class (there is an example on page 100 and many more at www.crownhouse. co.uk/featured/fun-mfl). Copy the vocabulary or phrases onto a PowerPoint slide and number each item (although not essential for this VFLA).
- Arrange your classroom seating plan so that you can divide the class into halves.
- Project the vocabulary or phrases onto the board so that every student can see them.

Instructions

- Hand out a mini-whiteboard, pen and eraser OR a piece of paper to all students in class.
- Ask the students to look at the projected list of vocabulary and write down six Target Language words and their English meaning in big, clear handwriting.
- Students who finish writing before others should rate each word according to their favourite sounding words, writing one to six (with one being their favourite and six being their least favourite) next to each word.
- Ask for three volunteers from each side of the class and tell them to bring their mini-whiteboard or paper to the front and to stand holding it so that the rest of the class can see it.
- Explain that when you say 'go' in the Target Language the seated students must put their heads on the desk with their eyes shut and their thumbs pointing upwards.
- Tell the students holding the mini-whiteboards or paper that they have twenty seconds to tweak the thumb of any student on the opposite team.
- They then return to the front of the class and hold up their mini-whiteboards or paper again.
- The students who have had their thumbs tweaked stand up and guess who they think tweaked their thumb by reading out the vocabulary held up by the person they thought did it.
- For every correct guess the teacher awards a point to that side.

Variations to the VFLA

- Vary the number of students chosen to carry out the thumb tweaking and have more than three per side. You could also vary the number of words to write down.

Teacher notes

If you are using mini-whiteboards then a good piece of advice suggested by Ross Morrison McGill in *100 Ideas for Secondary Teachers: Outstanding Lessons* is to get the tools (pens, erasers) attached to all the boards so that everything is kept together and you and the students are able to make efficient use of VFLA time.[20]

---

[20] McGill, (2013) p. 4.

Here's a vocab list in French to get you started (also available at www.crownhouse.co.uk/featured/fun–mfl)

1. *carte* = map OR menu OR card   *carte postale* = postcard
2. *auberge de jeunesse* = youth hostel
3. *gêné* = embarrassed / bothered
4. *faire du parapente* = to go paragliding
5. *feuilleton* = soap opera
6. *gagner de l'argent* = to earn money   *croisière* = cruise   *monde entier* = whole world
7. *côte* = coast
8. *tant pis!* = too bad!
9. *jumelles/jumeaux* = twins AND *jumelles* = binoculars
10. *institutrice/instituteur* = primary school teacher
11. *avoir confiance en* = to trust
12. *quand* AND *lorsque* = when
13. *être fort(e) en* = to be good / strong at   *être faible en* = to be weak at
14. *se disputer* = to argue   *dispute* = argument
15. *rencontrer* = to meet   *faire la connaissance de* = to meet (someone) OR to get to know (someone)   *se faire des amis* = to make friends
16. *avoir besoin de* = to need
17. *amitié* = friendship
18. *boulot* = job
19. *pas mal de monde* = quite a few people
20. *occupé* = busy
21. *boîte* AND *boîte de nuit* = nightclub
22. *incendie* = fire AND *feu* = fire OR traffic light   (*feu rouge* = red light)
23. *par jour/par nuit* = per day / per night
24. *rigoler/rire/rigolade* = ALL TO DO WITH LAUGHING   *sourire* = to smile
25. *s'entendre bien avec/s'entendre mal avec* = to get on well with / badly with
26. *repasser* = to iron   *vider les poubelles/le lave-vaisselle* = to empty the bins / dishwasher
27. *nettoyer* = to clean   *débarrasser la table* = to clear the table

Chapter 5

The Fun Learning Activities (FLAs)

Introduction

Not to be confused with the Foreign Language Assistant abbreviation, the FLAs are classroom teaching and learning tools, just like the VFLAs.

Each FLA is different: some take only ten or fifteen minutes, while others are designed to be whole lessons. Some are generic tools, some are short, snappy activities and others can be the basis for a whole sequence of lessons. The FLAs are not all skills based; there are some FLAs which also get the students practising language knowledge. A FLA might have elements of students working independently from the teacher, working collaboratively, demonstrating thinking skills, and applying knowledge.

All FLAs share four characteristics: they are fun, interesting, focused on the students' learning and assume that students already have some prior language knowledge, no matter how small.

The teacher decides which FLAs to incorporate into their teaching. They might plan to use one or two FLAs in one lesson and then to use a different FLA in another lesson later that week, half-term or term. FLAs are good rapport builders; by running a FLA with positivity, excitement, passion and enthusiasm it can help to bring the class and teacher together and build friendly, supportive and engaging relationships.

As with the VFLAs, talk about and refer to the FLAs by name, so that the students will also use the names and celebrate the fun and interest that they help generate.

Origins of the FLAs

During my first year of teaching, the school's teaching and learning vehicle was the Learning to Learn initiative underpinned by Paul Ginnis's *Teacher's Toolkit*.[1] I thought (and still think) that the tools were wonderful, especially the section where practical advice was given on how these tools might be adapted to suit different subjects in the curriculum. As I read through the description of each tool, I was desperate to try out all of the activities with as many classes as possible. Talking about creating a thirst for knowledge with our students, these tools created a thirst for more tools with me.

A few years later the school added the Teacher Effectiveness Enhancement Programme (TEEP) to its already impressive teaching and learning treasure chest. In helping the school promote this staff initiative, the excitement and buzz of having more activities to try out returned.

I am not claiming that the FLAs are all my original creations; some of my ideas came from watching great teachers and adapting the activities to suit language learning. Just as 'knowledge begets knowledge' for our students in the classroom, 'an inspirational idea begets an inspirational idea' for a teacher in the classroom. The FLA ideas are all a consequence of having taken the time to reflect on and think about my own practice. All the FLAs presented here have been thoroughly tested with my students.

Geoff Petty, in *Evidence-Based Teaching*, refers to 'methodological wars' and the debate between constructivist and behaviourist teaching methodologies.[2] The VFLAs are used to practise

---

[1] Ginnis, (2002).

[2] G. Petty, (2009) *Evidence-Based Teaching*, 2nd edition, Cheltenham, Nelson Thornes. pp. 101–102.

language knowledge ahead of retrieval, which falls under the latter methodology, but many features of the FLAs could be claimed to fall under the constructivist approach. After all, the teacher must decide when to use both VFLAs and FLAs. Bear in mind that both assume some level of prior knowledge upon which to build new learning.

There are 40 FLAs, all based on enjoyment, engagement and learning in a fun way. As with the VFLAs each FLA has a variations section and a teacher notes section.

I hope that you and your students enjoy them as much as my students and I have done.

1 Speak-Off (FLA)

The key idea behind the Speak-Off FLA is to support students in their speaking practice.

In *Debates in Modern Languages Education*, John Field suggests that automaticity is essential to being able to perform skilfully in a language.[3] Because novice speakers (and writers) in the classroom have to pay a lot of attention to detail in building their utterances, this places a huge demand on their working memories.

This FLA is about ways of dealing with students' inevitable 'hesitation pauses'.[4] Speaking a language means knowing not just about individual words, but also chunks of language – phrases, sayings, idioms and so on – which are used by native speakers. Learning such groups of words frees up space in working memory.[5] Having a repertoire of set phrases or sayings also supports the student in that their fluency (or automaticity) is increased, thus raising their confidence in speaking. In other words, students need to know set phrases.

For my A level French speaking test I memorised about eight reliable set phrases – 'fillers' I used to call them. I had already acquired a fair amount of language by then, but had not yet acquired the level of automaticity that I craved. These filler phrases gave me thinking time

---

3 Field in Driscoll et al., (2014) p. 23.

4 Field in Driscoll et al., (2014) p. 25.

5 Willingham, (2009) p. 34.

which allowed me to figure out what I was going to say next; they helped reduce my hesitation pauses. Admittedly, I said them fairly slowly while desperately searching for an actual point to make, rather than throwing another filler at the examiner with the equivalent of something like 'it is important that we take stock of the situation'.

On Edexcel's website it states that the changes include a 'focus on independent and spontaneous use of the Target Language'.[6] Therefore, you could support students who lack language automaticity by getting them to practise speaking using set phrases as chunks of language that they can see on the projected PowerPoint slide. Provide an image cue for each set phrase.

For example, if students are doing the Holidays topic (as described in the instructions below), find six holiday images (an airport, a campsite, a meal, the town centre, a tennis court, a mountain lake) and copy each image onto a PowerPoint slide. Add as many chunks of language related to each image as you would like students to practise. For a Spanish example, include sentences such as, *Me gusta pasar las vacaciones aquí porque me gustan las montañas* and *Normalmente me alojo en un camping porque está cerca del centro del pueblo.* In addition, underline any words which students could easily replace with others. For example, students could change *me gustan* to *me encantan.*

So that students have more language with which to practise give them a textbook with relevant vocabulary lists for the topic you are practising Speak-Off with. Students will then have both the chunk phrases on the PowerPoint as well as language from the textbook to support them.

Preparation and resources

- Identify the topic that you want students to practise language on; for example, Holidays or Healthy Living. Find six images to do with the topic and copy these onto a PowerPoint slide, leaving room to add language.
- Find ten or so useful Target Language chunk phrases to do with each image and type these onto the slide around the images.
- Arrange your classroom seating plan so that you can divide the class into pairs versus pairs.
- Project the Target Language chunk phrases and the first image onto the board so that every student can see them.
- Get a set of textbooks with a double page of vocabulary relevant to the topic.

---

[6] The first bullet point under Subject Content, on the page detailing a summary of the changes to the subject content at GCSE MFL for the new 2016 specifications: http://www.edexcel.com/subjects/Languages/Pages/ViewEditorial.aspx?editorial=1057.

Instructions

- Tell the class to get into pairs and say that each pair will be competing against another pair as pair A and pair B.
- Each pair needs to sit opposite another pair so that both half-face each other and half-face the board. They need to see each other and the chunks of language on the board.
- Give each pair a textbook open on the vocabulary pages for the topic.
- Explain that you are going to show an image to do with the topic and that a student in one pair will use the language on the board to help them talk about the image.
- Students must talk for two minutes with pair A starting. If the student speaking hesitates for more than five seconds then a student in the opposing pair takes over. If they hesitate for more than five seconds the turn passes back to the pair who started.
- The pair speaking at the end of two minutes wins the point.
- Students may use the Target Language chunks on the board and the language in the textbook, but can only repeat the same Target Language chunk four times.

Variations to the FLA

- Vary the time limit: have one minute instead of two minutes.
- Vary the hesitation pause length: have three seconds for a group at a higher level.
- Get the students to record each speak-off so that they can monitor what they've said later. John Field refers to this in *Debates in Modern Languages Education*.[7]
- Make Speak-Off a whole-lesson FLA. After two minutes get pairs doing Speak-Off against different pairs in class. Keep a record of the pairs that have won and lost against each other and update this throughout the lesson.

Teacher notes

The students will be speaking a lot of language with Speak-Off. Make sure that the pronunciation of set phrases and of any unfamiliar words has been modelled clearly. To save space on the PowerPoint slide, omit the English translations. In that case, make sure that the class are comfortable with the meaning of all the language on the slide.

There's obviously going to be a lot of repetition with Speak-Off and that's fine. Just make sure that the students are using Target Language chunks which are relevant to the image being spoken about.

---

[7] Field in Driscoll et al., (2014) p. 26.

2 Four Skills, Four Corners (FLA)

In Four Skills, Four Corners two groups of three or four students work on a listening task in one corner of the class, two groups engage in a speaking task in the second corner, two groups do a reading task in the third, and two groups work on a writing task in the remaining corner. Each group competes against the other groups to get the highest total from all four skills.

It's a carousel-based FLA with ten minutes spent on each skill. At the end of ten minutes the groups move clockwise around the room to complete the next task. For example, one group moves from the listening task to the speaking corner, and so on. At the end of forty minutes, all the groups have completed a task in every corner, leaving you just enough time in an hour-long lesson to go through the answers.

For FLAs which involve the students practising language in groups, I always have group roles assigned to the students. Jackie Beere, in *The Perfect Ofsted Lesson*, refers to the importance of allocating different responsibilities to various students as a way of getting them to work more effectively.[8] For this FLA, allocate the following roles: dictionary researcher (consults the dictionary), textbook researcher (checks the textbook), scribe (does the writing) and leader (oversees the process).

By the way, whenever a FLA mentions students adopting a role within the group, this doesn't mean that they only perform this role. The whole group is expected to work towards the

---

8 Beere, (2012) p. 95.

group's aim; the assigned roles indicate what they should be doing *in addition to* working towards the group goal. Assigning roles also helps you to question students as to what their role is should they appear off-task in a group.

In choosing a task for each corner, be as creative as you wish. For example, I've used a past paper question for the reading and the listening corners, a set of six pictures on a storyboard as a prompt for the speaking corner, and a set of five short sentences to translate for the writing corner. The reading and writing tasks could be on pieces of paper; the listening corner needs some devices for playing the material; and the speaking corner needs a means for enabling students to record themselves.

Once the students have completed the tasks in the four different corners, as a class you will mark the groups' efforts to determine the winners. That's the Four Skills, Four Corners FLA.

Preparation and resources

- For the listening corner set up two CD players ready to play a past listening paper question.
- For the speaking corner make two copies of a storyboard template with six pictures on it. Leave the captions underneath blank. Put two Dictaphones in this corner.
- For the writing corner, make two copies of a handout of five English sentences to translate.
- For the reading corner, make two copies of a past reading paper.
- Arrange your classroom seating plan so that there is enough space at each corner in the classroom for a maximum of eight students (two groups of four students) to work.
- Put enough dictionaries, textbooks, paper and pens at each corner for the groups to work with.
- Project onto the board what the task that the students have to do in each corner is.

Instructions

- Tell the class to get into groups of three or four and to assign the roles of dictionary researcher, textbook researcher, scribe and leader. Explain the roles as described above.
- Tell two groups to stand at the listening corner, two groups to stand at the speaking corner, two groups to stand at the reading corner and two groups to stand at the writing corner.
- Explain that each group has to work together to complete the task at their corner and that there will be a ten-minute time limit for this. Apart from the speaking corner, the groups complete their task on the paper provided.

- At the end of ten minutes, the students take their answer with them (apart from at the speaking corner where they leave the Dictaphone) and move in a clockwise direction to the next corner where they will work on the next task.
- When at the listening corner, the students listening to a past paper question can play, pause and replay the CD as necessary for writing their answer.
- At the speaking corner students record their storyboard answers on the Dictaphones; at the reading corner and writing corner students will put their answers on paper.
- Once all of the groups have visited every corner you will go through the answers as a class with each group marking another group's answers. The group with the most correct answers wins Four Skills, Four Corners.

Variations to the FLA

- Change the tasks in the corner. Instead of a past listening paper question, set up a listening exercise from the textbook or get your foreign language assistant to record a short passage of listening material and use this.
- Instead of four different skills then have the same skill but a different task for that skill in each corner. Having a different listening task or speaking task would require more equipment being available but it is certainly still doable.

Teacher notes

If you're struggling for time in the lesson then don't squeeze in the marking of the completed tasks in the same lesson. Put it off until next time. The receptive skills of reading and listening can be marked quite quickly by showing the class the answers, but it will probably take longer to mark the speaking tasks.

3 Relay (FLA)

Relay is a way of measuring students' progress, and at one time I used to do Relay every lesson. It provides instant feedback for the students on their ability to translate short sentences.

Let's suppose that the students have been learning to describe hair and eye colour and giving physical descriptions using the Target Language for sentences such as, 'I have brown hair', 'I have blue eyes' and 'I am quite tall'.

Prepare a dozen or so sets of numbered English sentences such as:

1. I have brown hair.
2. I have blue eyes.
3. I am quite tall.
4. I am quite small.
5. I have a beard.
6. I wear glasses.

Put each sentence on a separate strip of paper. The students form groups of three or four and assign the following roles: scribe (does the writing), runner (takes the translation to you) and two researchers (who consult dictionaries and textbooks).

Go round to each group and hand them the first strip turned over so they can't see the English. When you say 'go', they turn over the first sentence and work together to help the scribe write the Target Language translation for the English. Once the group is happy with the translation they send the runner to you with the sentence for checking. If it's not 100% perfect then give a little feedback to the runner on what they can do to fix it and send them back to their group to work on it.

When a runner brings a sentence that has been translated perfectly give them the next sentence for their group to work on. Groups can only move onto the next sentence once their current sentence has been checked and passed as 100% perfect. The Relay winner is the group that completes all of the sentences first.

In the Relay FLA, the nature of the short sentences to translate each time means that you can focus on very specific areas of the language that students have got wrong. Here, the students are getting immediate feedback and acting on it. Lemov says that people should be in a position to practise putting feedback to use as quickly as possible,[9] and the feedback needs to be specific.[10]

Because you are feeding back to one student in a group (the runner), explain to the class how important it is to choose a runner who is able to communicate your feedback to the rest of their group accurately.

Preparation and resources

- Identify the topic that you want students to practise language on. For example, Physical Descriptions as above.
- Choose six English sentences that translate some of the Target Language that the students have been using in class and type these onto a document.
- Make enough copies of the document to match the number of groups.
- Cut up the six sentences so that you have one set of the sentences for each group.
- Although not essential, arrange your classroom seating plan so that it allows the groups to work so that they are facing each other in a base.

Instructions

- Tell the class to get into groups of three or four and to assign the following roles: scribe, runner, and one or two (if a group of four) researchers.

---

[9] Lemov, (2012) p. 120.

[10] D. Didau, (2014) *The Secret of Literacy: Making the Implicit, Explicit*, Carmarthen, Independent Thinking Press. p. 197.

- Explain that you have prepared six English sentences for each group to translate and that you are going to give each group a copy of just the first sentence turned over (so they can't see the English).
- When you say 'go' groups turn their copy over and work together to translate it into the Target Language; the scribe does the writing and the other group members help according to their roles.
- Once a group is happy with their translation they send their runner with it to you at the front of the class.
- If it has been translated perfectly you will give the runner the next sentence to take back to their group to translate.
- If it is not translated perfectly give the runner feedback on how to improve it and send them back to their group so they can fix it. After fixing it, they must return to have it checked.
- The group can only move on to the next sentence when their runner has shown you a perfect version of their group's translation. The winning group is the one to complete all six sentences first.

Variations to the FLA

- Use Target Language sentences to translate into English.
- Use sets of vocabulary to translate instead of sentences.
- Use short paragraphs to translate. Give the paragraphs out in a different order from how they would appear as a whole text so that once students have completed the relay then they have to put these into the correct sequence.
- Use Target Language sentences with mistakes in and students have to find and correct the mistakes.
- Use Target Language sentences with mistakes in and students have to find and correct the mistakes and then translate them.
- Choose two students (already briefed on the content of the rights and wrongs of the language used in the relay) to act as teacher-students to run the relay instead of you. Have them sitting at the front of the class for runners to come to.
- Use a past reading paper as the content for Relay as a way of initiating students into the world of exams. Expose them to how they will eventually be assessed using a fun group activity (as opposed to giving individual students the onerous task of completing a paper by themselves under timed conditions in class). For this variation, tell the groups that they must not move on to the next question on the past paper until you have checked that they have got full marks for the current question. Incidentally, if a group doesn't get full marks on a question then when their runner comes back to you to check their answer a second time have them explain why they have put down their new answer. This justification avoids students simply guessing.

- Allow some groups dictionaries and others not; introduce a rule that this is rotated amongst the class or apply this variation in a mixed ability class. Vary the challenge for each group within the class so a more dominant group has to work without a dictionary.
- Give Target Language sentences to translate into English for certain groups and English into Target Language for other groups during the same relay.
- Use grammar exercises (like gap-fills) to complete, with students not being allowed to go onto the second exercise without having got the first correct.
- When feeding back to the runner on their group's mistakes, you could just tell them the number of mistakes they have made but not what they are. This method is suggested in *Modern Foreign Languages: Inside the Black Box* as a way of encouraging the students to act on the feedback.[11] This would work well if you were running the Relay FLA using a set of sentences with deliberate mistakes in where the students had to find and correct these mistakes.

Teacher notes

The Relay FLA can work in pairs but with a big class things can get a bit busy for you and a queue of runners can sometimes accumulate at your desk.

---

[11] Jones and Wiliam, (2008) p. 14.

4 Statement Stand-Up (FLA)

In this FLA students stand up if they agree with a statement you make in the Target Language. It's a quick, simple FLA you could use at any point during a lesson to recap prior learning, and to check students' understanding.

Suppose that the students are learning about siblings and families. You make a statement in the Target Language, such as, *J'ai un frère*. Those students in the class who have a brother stand up. You make another statement, *J'ai deux sœurs*, and those who have two sisters stand up, and so on.

It's a good idea to ask those students who haven't stood up, 'Why did they stand up?' and get them to reply by using the 'he/she' form of the verb in the Target Language.

With a class trained in the Target Language and familiar with this FLA, a possible exchange could go something like this:

Teacher: *J'ai deux frères.*

(Those students with two brothers stand up. The teacher then selects a student who is sitting down and points to a student standing up).

Teacher: *Est-ce que tu peux expliquer?*

Student: *Parce qu'il a deux frères.*

You could then double check that the class have understood by getting a student who stood up to explain in English why they stood up.

Preparation and resources

- Identify the topic that you want to practise with the students; for example, Family, Hobbies or Sports. Find ten (or so) statements to do with the topic and copy these statements (Target Language only) onto a PowerPoint slide.
- No specific classroom layout is required.
- Project the statements onto the board so that every student can see them.

Instructions

- Explain to the class that you are going to speak a Target Language sentence on the projected PowerPoint slide.
- If the sentence you call out describes them personally (for example, what brothers and sisters they have) then they have to stand up until you tell them to sit down again.
- You will check on why students have stood up or have remained seated by asking them to explain (following the model above).
- Ask the students to sit back down and then speak a different Target Language sentence on the board.

Variations to the FLA

- Instead of you providing the statements for the students, give them ten minutes or so to come up with some of the language they have learned so far in this lesson or the past few lessons and use these as the statements. For example, suppose the students had been learning about the environment. They spend ten minutes writing down statements about how people support the environment, and you project or write them on the board. The statements could be basic statements about what people should do in order to help the environment like, 'We should plant more trees.' and 'We should recycle paper.' You then read out a statement and if a student does that then they stand up.
- You don't have to project the sentences on the board. Try speaking sentences in the Target Language which have been covered recently to see how much they recognise.
- Get the students running the FLA themselves in groups of four or five with one student acting as teacher-student, speaking the sentences.

- Any statements about characteristics that the students might share can work: hair and eye colour, food and drink, school subjects, and so on.
- You could even have a set of half-statements projected on the board, like *Je joue au foot,* with those students standing up having to add to your sentence using an opinion phrase such as *parce que c'est génial.*

Teacher notes

If you project the language onto the board then try to cover all the language terms that could possibly apply to the students. For example, with statements about family include words to do with parents and step-parents, half-brothers and half-sisters, or grandparents, to ensure you don't leave anyone out.

5 Stand Up Sit Down (FLA)

There was a time when most of my lessons would begin with Stand Up Sit Down, which I used as a way of getting students thinking about the language coming up in the lesson. I loved using it as a way of getting a class fired up for their learning.

Type a short Target Language paragraph onto a PowerPoint slide, underlining the words and short phrases that you want to draw the students' attention to. Project the paragraph onto the board and read it out three times, each time more quickly than the last.

When you read out the first underlined word or phrase the class stands up, when you read the next one the class sits down, the next one they stand up again, and so on, to the end of the paragraph. Why do this? Because I'm for anything that gets students moving about.

Using this FLA at the start of a new topic or new grammar point is a way of priming the students to make a connection between the language underlined and the content of the lesson to come. After the students sit down following the third run through of the paragraph ask them, 'What do you think we'll be learning about today? How do you know? Why have I underlined these particular phrases?'

In *How Learning Works: Seven Research-Based Principles for Smart Teaching* the authors refer to students learning and retaining more when they can connect what they are learning to prior knowledge: 'new knowledge "sticks" better when it has prior knowledge to stick to'.[12] Even

---

[12] S. A. Ambrose, M. W. Bridges, M. DiPietro, M. C. Lovett, M. K. Norman and R. E. Mayer, (2010) *How Learning Works: Seven Research-Based Principles for Smart Teaching*, San Francisco, Jossey-Bass. p. 15.

though I usually use this FLA with a new language topic, whenever I prepare a paragraph for Stand Up Sit Down I focus on some aspect of the language that the students will already be familiar with, giving them enough cues to allow them an insight into the material I'm presenting. The example below is built upon students' prior knowledge of the words *geography* and *maths* in English. Cognates work well as a cue to allow students to access a text more easily with this FLA.

This FLA works well with a Target Language explanation of the instructions.

> *Me encanta <u>la educación física</u> pero no me gusta <u>el inglés</u>. Me gusta <u>la geografía</u> porque es interesante. Odio <u>las ciencias</u> pero me encantan <u>las matemáticas</u>.*

Preparation and resources

- Identify the topic that you want to introduce to the students. This could be School Subjects, as in the shaded section above. Type out a Target Language paragraph onto a PowerPoint slide and underline four or five words or short phrases (cognates work well) which will allow students to connect the language that you read out to their prior knowledge.
- No specific classroom layout is needed.
- Project the paragraph onto the board so that every student can see it.

Instructions

- Explain that you are going to read the paragraph on the board three times with each time being quicker than the previous time.
- When you read out the first underlined word or short phrase the class should stand up and stay standing up until you read the next underlined word or short phrase out, when they sit back down again.
- Continue to read out the paragraph. When the students hear the next underlined word or short phrase they alternately stand up and sit down again.
- Read the paragraph twice more, but more quickly each time.

Variations to the FLA

- The first two times keep the paragraph hidden. Before starting the FLA, pronounce the words in the paragraph that you want the students to stand up and sit down to. The third time through, show the students the paragraph, and afterwards discuss how they imagined the paragraph would be written.
- Use the FLA as a fast dictation. Prepare the FLA to do midway through a topic in a Scheme of Learning, but don't project the paragraph. Then explain that the students will have to rely on their prior knowledge of the language covered in the topic so far to write down any words or phrases that they hear (but not see) you read out. (You might have to do this more than three times.)
- Use the FLA towards the end of a lesson and then use Relay (FLA #3) to complete a translation of the text you've used for Stand Up Sit Down.
- If a class is familiar with Stand Up Sit Down, first project a paragraph with nothing underlined and discuss with the students which words and phrases they think should be underlined and why. Then run the FLA.
- Model the pronunciation of the paragraph, then get a confident student to do the reading while you take their place in class to join in the FLA.
- Students create a paragraph in a lesson to be used in the following lesson as the Stand Up Sit Down FLA. This also works well to connect to prior learning.

Teacher notes

Make sure that the students know you will not pause during the reading of the paragraph. So, the first time through read it at normal speed (observing students standing up and sitting back down as you read it), the next time a little more quickly, and finally rapid fire. However, as a cheeky, rapport-building tactic (and I'm about to contradict what I've just written), on the last speedy read-through I like to pause just before reading out an underlined word or phrase.

Students may ask if they stand up when you say the *el* or *la* or the actual word for the school subject. It's as soon as you start reading the underlined word or phrase that they stand up.

6 Teacher vs. YouTube (FLA)

This FLA is designed to promote a discussion with your students about how they learn best: visual-based media vs. direct instruction. In *Visible Learning*, Hattie says visual-based learning has very small effect sizes.[13] This is important for the Teacher vs. YouTube FLA because here you are effectively conducting a study with your class in order to prove that a video clip is no match for you. One side of the class is taught a new tense through direct teacher instruction whilst the other side is taught it through the medium of YouTube. After running the FLA, you discuss the relative merits of your own teaching and feedback compared to that of the instructional quality of a video clip – which is better? I would only run this FLA with a class with whom I had a good rapport.

Find a clip on YouTube which, while still being new learning, references what you know the students already know. For example, if the students know what an infinitive is then make sure that the clip has several references to infinitives.

Split the class into halves and explain that one side will be taught by YouTube and the other side taught by you. Ask the class, 'Who wants to be taught by me?' (I dare you.) Then explain that both sides have to make notes on the conjugation of the tense, when it's used and the common irregular verb formations.

---

[13] J. Hattie, (2009) *Visible Learning: A Synthesis of Over 800 Meta-Analyses Relating to Achievement*, Abingdon, Routledge. pp. 229–230.

The YouTube side faces the board and you play the clip for them. Ask one student to operate the clip. They have to make notes on tense formation, usage and any irregularities. They can pause and rewind the clip as and when they like. You teach the other side the same content, but from the back of the classroom, which means the students turn their backs to the YouTube clip. Stick up a piece of MWB on the back wall to write on.

The whole teaching process involving both sides takes no longer than fifteen minutes followed by a test. Students' scores from both sides are totalled to see which side wins out of the Teacher and YouTube.

After the fifteen minutes of instruction, test the students with both sides facing the board. Project a set of twelve or so sentences as a gap-fill exercise to assess their ability in conjugating the tense that has just been taught. For example, the first sentence on the gap-fill could be:

1.   *Hier, nous* _____ _____ (*manger*)

Students complete all the gap-fill sentences, which are then marked by students on the opposite side.

Now, calculate the result. Add up the individual scores to give you the total per side (discount one score if the teams are unequal, or find the average score). However, the result matters less than the discussion that takes place after the winning side has been determined. This discussion about teaching methods, how and why the students have learned best, is more important than the summative-type grade effect of one side doing better.

Preparation and resources

- Identify the tense that you would like to teach to the students. Find a YouTube clip which teaches the same information about the tense: when it's used and which verbs have irregular forms and so on.
- Stick a piece of MWB up at the back of the class.
- Arrange your classroom seating plan so that you can divide the class into front and back.
- Set the YouTube clip up so that it is ready to play on the projector.

Instructions

- Explain to the class that they are going to work as one side against the other. One side will face the board and be taught a new tense by a YouTube clip. The other side will be taught by you on a MWB at the back of the room (with their backs to the YouTube clip).

- Whichever way they are taught, every student makes notes on the tense. These notes should include: tense formation, when it's used and if the tense has any irregular forms.
- The students watching the clip can pause and rewind it as many times as they like. As the teaching will take fifteen minutes then students watching the clip will need to manage the time accordingly. Ask one student to control the playback.
- After the teaching there will be a test on the tense so they need to make accurate notes.
- Play the clip and teach the tense. Project the gap-fill sentences and get the students to complete them. Get them to swap their books with students on the opposing side, project the answers and get the students to mark them.
- Add up the scores and decide on a winner between you and YouTube. Discuss with the students the effectiveness of each teaching approach.

Variations to the FLA

- Vary what you teach each side. Instead of a verb tense find a clip on another aspect of grammar, such as adjectives.
- Vary how long you teach your side for and how long the other side can watch the clip for.
- Run the FLA with two different classes simultaneously. Have one class watching the clip of a tense in one classroom and another class being taught the tense by their teacher in another classroom. Then do the same test with both classes and discuss the results. The following lesson repeat the process with a different tense and groups being taught the opposite way: the class who were taught by the teacher last time are now taught by the YouTube clip, and vice versa. Test again and ask the class to compare their experiences of both ways of being taught.

Teacher notes

Speak reasonably quietly to the students who are sitting with their backs to the board; ensure the sound of the clip is also kept at a reasonable volume, so that there is minimum interference.

You could play the clip as a Scene-Setter (FLA #40) for the students and have it playing as they enter the classroom to provoke curiosity.

In the following lesson teach the tense again to ensure that all students have understood it and then get the students to use that tense in context and thus apply their knowledge. Get them to translate some sentences to build a Target Language paragraph.

This can be a great rapport builder too. Depending on the clip you choose on YouTube, you and the class can compare and contrast your teaching style with that of the YouTube teacher.

7 Interrogation (FLA)

My first live experience of hot seating occurred as an NQT on a cross-curricular lesson observation programme. In that history lesson a student was brought out to the front and asked various questions about the content they had covered.

I tried a version of hot seating using questions in the Target Language about basic personal details. One student sat at the front and was asked various questions: *'¿Cómo te llamas?'*, *'¿Tienes hermanos?'*. As an activity it was OK, but it didn't involve enough of the class, creating the familiar problem of what everyone else in the class was doing while two students were involved in asking and answering questions.

So I changed the activity to include a student from each side of the class sitting at the front, facing the rest of the class with their backs to the board. Then I projected a list of numbered questions on the board so that the rest of the class could see what they were going to ask the two students.

In order to involve the whole class I explained that whenever a question was asked by any student then the whole class would write down the number of that question and put a tick or a cross next to it according to whether or not they could answer it themselves.

The side versus side competitive element arose by having the two students at the front come from each side of the class and sit facing the opposite side. Each side would then take it in turns to ask the student facing them one of the questions on the board. However, sides could not repeat a question they had already asked, nor could they ask the same question the other side had just used, to avoid having the answer already modelled by the other student.

When the student answered a question, I wrote up the name of the student, the number of the question asked and put a tick or a cross next to the number depending on how well it was answered (according to my judgment!). The rest of the class would also write the number of the question and put a tick or a cross according to whether they could answer it themselves. The process was then repeated with the student on the other side and so on until both students had been asked five questions each.

The winning student was the one who had the most ticks for questions answered correctly. If there was a draw then a question penalty shoot-out ensued. Once the winning student had been crowned Interrogation Champion the rest of the class had a record of which questions they could and couldn't answer.

As a refinement, I've got the students in pairs to make a list of the questions that they couldn't answer and then test each other on them.

Preparation and resources

- Identify the group of Target Language questions and answers that you want to practise with a class. For example, a list of questions to do with personal details, as the following example. Copy the questions onto a PowerPoint slide and number each item.
- Arrange your classroom seating plan to divide the class into two and put two chairs up front facing each half of the class.
- Project the questions onto the board.

1. *¿Cómo te llamas?*
2. *¿Cuántos años tienes?*
3. *¿Cuándo es tu cumpleaños?*
4. *¿Tienes animales en casa?*
5. *¿Tienes hermanos?*
6. *¿Dónde vives?*
7. *¿De dónde eres?*
8. *¿Cómo eres?*

Instructions

- Ask for two student volunteers, one from each side of the class, and have them sit on chairs facing the opposite side from which they have just come.

- Tell the class that these students will be under interrogation. Write the name of each student on a whiteboard.
  - Explain that this is a side versus side activity, and that each side will take turns to ask the student facing them any of the questions projected on the board.
  - One student asks a question of the student in the hot seat. If they answer correctly then write the number of the question and a tick next to it underneath their name on the whiteboard. If the student gives an incorrect response put a cross.
  - Whenever a question is asked, the rest of the class must also write the number of the question and put a tick or a cross depending on whether they could answer it themselves.
  - Explain that they cannot be asked the same question more than once, nor can the same question be put to both sides consecutively; a different question has to be asked in between.
  - The winning student, the Interrogation Champion, is the one with the most ticks out of five.

Variations to the FLA

- Instead of questions, project Target Language sentences that the students under interrogation have to translate into English, or vice versa. You can still get the rest of the class involved: they write the number of the sentence and a tick or a cross according to if they could translate it correctly or not. You could ask the rest of the class if they think the student under interrogation has got the translation correct before confirming one way or the other.
- Vary the number of students under interrogation. Have two students from each side at the front (supporting one another).
- Get the students in the rest of the class to put their ticks and crosses on mini-whiteboards and to show you their own response each time a student under interrogation answers.
- At a higher level, such as A level, use the FLA with more evaluative questions and set a minimum time limit that students must be able to speak for in order to get a tick for a question answered fully.
- Introduce a time limit for the students under interrogation to provide an answer.

Teacher notes

An extension to the FLA is to get the students to deal with the ticks and crosses that they have put down. Once the Interrogation Champion has been decided, the class swap over their answer sheets (or mini-whiteboards) and list the questions to which their partner needs an answer. The two students under interrogation could also do the same based on the questions and answers that they got right and wrong. Make sure that you discuss with the whole class why you have given a tick or a cross for the student under interrogation's response.

8 Mobile Phun (FLA)

This is a good way of practising a short dialogue or a question and answer. It is a version of Pass the Parcel, except that the two parcels are actually laminated enlarged pictures of a mobile phone.

Split the class into two sides and give one mobile cut-out to each side. Explain that you will start the FLA by playing some music and you want each side to pass the mobile amongst the students on their side. When you stop the music, the students holding the mobiles have to stand up. The first to do so asks a Target Language question of the other standing student who gives an appropriate response.

To add a greater incentive for asking and answering questions, I award a point if the student asks a question within two seconds of me stopping the music, and if the other student responds within two seconds.

When running this FLA in the past I've projected onto the board all of the language covered in the topic; for example, in the Making Invitations topic I used language from questions such as '*Tu veux aller au cinéma?*' and responses to the invitations, such as, '*D'accord*' or '*Bonne idée.*' Of course, without projecting any language on the board you can find out what the students can recall.

Preparation and resources

- Make two mobile phone laminates (two soft toys will work just as well).
- Identify the topic you want to practise with a class. Choose a topic that fits well with the question and answer theme; for example, arranging to go out, or deciding what to

eat or wear. Copy some of the likely questions and answers onto a PowerPoint slide as a support.

- Arrange your classroom seating plan to divide the class into halves.
- Project the questions and answers onto the board so that every student can see them.

Instructions

- Explain that this FLA is like Pass the Parcel and that you will give each side of the class a mobile phone (or soft toy).
- You will play some music and each side will pass the mobile to each other within their half of the class.
- When you stop the music, the students on each side of the class holding the mobile stand up.
- The first to stand up must ask a Target Language question to the other student standing, who must then give an appropriate Target Language response to that question.
- If the question is asked within two seconds or the response is given within two seconds, then you will award a point as appropriate.
- Start the music again, the students sit and pass the mobiles to the next student, and so on.

Variations to the FLA

- Show pictures on the board instead of language. The students with their mobiles stand up and describe the picture. The student who is able to sustain their description of the picture the longest wins the point for their side. (If a student copies the other student then it is quite obvious and it is the other student who wins. The rest of the class remain fairly quiet so that you can hear them speak.)
- Students holding the mobiles stand up and nominate someone else from their side to speak.

Teacher notes

This FLA can work well when getting the students to practise a dialogue, for instance, one between a doctor and a patient, or a shop assistant and a shopper. Prepare some dialogues earlier in the lesson; the students then adapt the language to the current situation. The dialogue has to be as spontaneous as possible.

9 PCs (FLA)

This FLA creates a dialogue between a 'police constable' and a 'criminal.' It's a good rapport builder with a class as well as practising questions and answers in the Target Language. It works best with questions which have a range of possible answers. Start by teaching the question, '*Quelle est la date de ton anniversaire?*' to a class and get them to write '*Mon anniversaire, c'est le …* ' with their own birthday.

Find a date that no student in the class has as their birthday. Write this on the board in the Target Language. This date is going to be the criminal's birthday. Ask for a volunteer from each side of the class and give them a plastic police helmet each. While this is optional, props such as police helmets and the like are always good rapport builders with a class. Indeed, Amy Buttner suggests that a prop box is an essential component to a languages classroom.[14] These two students will be the PCs and it will be their job to find out who the criminal is: it is the student who says the birthday date on the board and not their own birthday. Explain that whichever of the PCs finds this student first by hearing them speak this date wins a point for their side. The PCs then leave the room and you decide who the criminal will be.

When the PCs return they will ask each student in turn the key question, '*Quelle est la date de ton anniversaire?*' and wait for their answer. If they are not given the criminal's date, they move on to ask another student. The PCs work individually and not as a pair as they are competing against each other. Once one of the PCs has 'arrested' the criminal, choose two more PCs and a new criminal, and repeat.

---

[14] A. Buttner, (2007) *Activities, Games, Assessment Strategies, and Rubrics For The Foreign Language Classroom*, Abingdon, Routledge. p. 3.

Preparation and resources

- Get two plastic police helmets (or other similar props).
- Identify the Target Language question and the kinds of answers that you want to practise with a class. For example, this could be one key question to do with birthdays or it could be one from a set of four or five questions to do with a topic. Copy the question(s) onto a PowerPoint slide.
- Arrange your classroom seating plan to divide the class into halves.
- Project the question(s) onto the board so that every student can see them.

Instructions

- Explain to the class that they are going to write an answer to a Target Language question that you show them. Model an answer first and get every student to write their own answer.
- Find an answer to the Target Language question that no student in class has written down by asking 'Has anyone put down *x*?' until you find an answer that no one has. This becomes the criminal's answer; write this on the board. If the Target Language question is, 'When is your birthday?' then the criminal's answer is a date that no other student in the class has.
- Ask for two student volunteers, one from each side of the class, and tell them that they will be the PCs. Give them a police helmet each.
- Send the PCs out, then choose a student to be the criminal. Call the PCs back in and observe them asking each student the Target Language question until the first PC to ask and hear the criminal's answer wins.

Variations to the FLA

- Vary the number of PCs you send out.
- Vary the number of criminals you have.
- Have a different Target Language question each time you run this FLA.
- Instead of a question and answer format choose a pair of students to be the criminal pair speaking the criminal's dialogue. All students in the class speak a dialogue they have designed themselves repeatedly until a PC finds the pair speaking the criminal's dialogue.
- At a higher level you could provide a list of topics, and choose the topic for the criminals to discuss. The PCs then listen to pairs discussing a variety of topics and 'arrest' the students who are discussing the criminal topic.

Teacher notes

To ensure that more students play more of an active role I have also run the FLA as a survey. Keep the PCs but have the rest of the class asking each other the key question, and listening to each other's answers. This version of the FLA takes a little longer for the PCs to find out who the criminals are because they have to listen to pairs during the survey rather than them being able to ask students directly.

10 Screwed-Up Exercises (FLA)

This FLA is all about randomising tasks that students set for each other to work on in groups.

Project a list of possible exercises that the students could complete on the board as in the following example. Ensure that the selection of tasks come from topics which have already been covered with the group so that they are practising familiar language.

1. Complete Exercise 2b Page 23
2. Complete Exercise 5b Page 28
3. Complete Exercise 3b Page 29
4. Complete Exercise 4c Page 32
5. Complete Exercise 2a Page 32
6. Complete Exercise 1c Page 27
7. Complete Exercise 1d Page 32
8. Complete Exercise 4b Page 18
9. Complete Exercise 2a Page 22
10. Complete Exercise 1d Page 15
11. Complete Exercise 2d Page 31
12. Complete Exercise 1c Page 30
13. Complete Exercise 3a Page 25
14. Complete Exercise 2c Page 16
15. Complete Exercise 2b Page 29
16. Complete Exercise 1a Page 35

The students work in groups of three and assign the standard roles of scribe, textbook researcher, and dictionary researcher/runner. (With groups of four separate the dictionary researcher/ runner into two roles). The groups first decide upon a group name. They then choose five different exercises from the list, write them on two separate scrap pieces of paper, screw up the papers and put them into a box at the front of the class. The result is a box full of double the number of screwed-up pieces of paper as there are groups.

Each group finds a base in the classroom. When you say the Target Language word for 'go' they each send their runner (forming an orderly queue!) to collect a screwed-up task. The runner returns to their group, unfolds the task and the group selects one of the five exercises to complete. The groups complete exercises in books or on the MWB. When a group thinks they have done an exercise correctly, you check it. If it's correct they win a point and note this down. If the task is not correct, give them some guidance on what to do. When a group completes a task correctly they tick it off on the scrap paper and write the group's name next to it. Then they screw the paper up again and the runner returns to the box, rummages for another screwed-up piece of paper to take back to their group, and returns the previous one to the box. The group then completes a different task.

The first group to complete five exercises which have all been checked by you wins the FLA.

Preparation and resources

- Identify some exercises and their page references from the textbook (from any modules already covered). Put the number of each exercise and the page reference onto one slide as in the example on page 131.
- To avoid students copying from others it's probably better not to stick MWBs up around the room, so just make them available on the desks at each group's base.
- Put a box at the front of the class for the screwed-up papers.
- No specific seating plan is required for this FLA but you might want to arrange it so that groups of three can work together on a MWB at a base on a set of desks.
- Project the slide with the exercises on the board so that every student can see it.

Instructions

- Explain to the class that they are going to work in groups of three competing against other groups to complete exercises from the textbook.
- Each group assigns the following roles: scribe, textbook researcher, dictionary researcher/runner. Explain the roles as described above.

- Each group finds a base in the classroom and chooses a name.
- They have two pieces of scrap paper on which they copy any five exercises from the list on the board. They then screw up the papers and put them in the box at the front.
- Explain that when you say the Target Language cue-word for 'go' each group sends their runner to the box at the front to collect a screwed-up piece of paper and bring it back to their group.
- The groups work together to complete the exercise, calling you over when they think they have completed it correctly. If it's correct they gain a point. If it's incorrect give them some help.
- If the exercise is correct, the group must tick the exercise on the paper, write their group name in brackets and then send the runner to fetch another screwed-up piece of paper from the box at the front and return the previous one.
- This process continues until the group with five points (five correct exercises) wins.

Variations to the FLA

- Vary the number of exercises.
- Vary how students can win a point. Award teacher discretionary points to groups who use consistently good Target Language, groups who are working well as a team, etc.
- Introduce counters for students to use if they need to 'buy' an explanation.
- Instead of textbook tasks prepare grammar exercises to complete.

Teacher notes

There should be no need for any extension tasks here since the exercises just keep arriving by runner from the box at the front. The groups should always be working on an exercise until a group gets to five points.

11 Mexican Crazy Card Wave (FLA)

Unsurprisingly, the Mexican Crazy Card Wave FLA is similar to the Mexican Wave (VFLA #4). In both, students in turn bob up and speak out a sentence in the Target Language. The key difference is that instead of projecting the language on the board, you make a class set of cards which have both a Target Language statement and a question. Each question is answered by another card. So, using the example on page 135, each card would have a past tense statement/answer such as *J'ai mangé le pain,* and a question beneath such as *Qui a mangé la pomme?* That question would be answered by another card, *J'ai mangé la pomme.* The accompanying question on that card, *Qui a mangé la cerise?* leads to yet another card and so on.

Make the pack of cards, shuffle them, and give one to each student. The student with just the question on their card begins the FLA. The student who can supply the answer to that question stands up, speaks the answer and asks the next question. They remain standing. The answering student repeats the process, and so on, until all the class are standing up. This differs from the Mexican Wave VFLA in that the students stand up randomly around the class – this is the 'Crazy' part of the name.

Although some initial preparation is required, this is a resource which you can always rely on thereafter.

It's important with the Mexican Card Wave to get the students competing against the clock.

Preparation and resources

- Identify the vocabulary topic and grammar point that you want to practise. The example below illustrates how you could get the students practising the perfect tense in the 'I' form on the topic of Food.
- Make a class set of small cards which have an answer and question to be answered by the next card as shown below. Ensure that the first card to start has just a question at the top. One card in the set will have just an answer, and this will be the last card.

Qui a mangé le pain?	*J'ai mangé le pain.* *Qui a mangé la pomme?*	*J'ai mangé la pomme.* *Qui a mangé la cerise?*
J'ai mangé la banane. *Qui a mangé la pêche?*	*J'ai mangé l'orange.* *Qui a mangé la banane?*	*J'ai mangé la cerise.* *Qui a mangé l'orange?*

Instructions

- Explain that the whole class is going to do a Mexican wave in a random order with cards and you are going to time the class to see how quickly they do it.
- Mix up the cards and hand one to every student in class. If there are more cards than students then give some of the more confident students two cards.
- The student who has the first card with just the question at the top begins by standing up and asking the question. Start the timer. The student remains standing.
- The student who has the card with the answer to this question stands up, speaks the answer, asks the question on their card, and remains standing.
- The process continues until every student is standing. Stop the timer.
- Mix the cards up and run the FLA again to see if the class can beat the time on their second attempt.

Variations to the FLA

- Once the last student has stood up and read from their card, repeat the FLA but with the students speaking what is on their card and then sitting back down and time the FLA in reverse.

- Divide a text up into sentences, put each sentence onto a card and number the cards in the order the sentences follow one another in the text. Run the FLA with students standing and speaking out their sentence on the card.

Teacher notes

If some students have been given two cards explain that they just speak out their answer and question. They don't have to sit down and stand back up again!

12 Painting The Preterite Tense (FLA)

Of course, this FLA can be used with any tense, not just the preterite – Painting The Present Tense, Painting The Perfect Tense – nor does the name of the tense have to begin with the letter *p*.

Once a group is familiar with regular tense formation, such as the preterite tense in Spanish, their task is to find a way of representing this tense formation using a limited number of symbols, letters, numbers and words. This has to be done in as creative a way as possible. Each group gives a brief thirty-second or one-minute explanation of how their representation of the tense works on a MWB.

The result is that you have a class of thirty students working in groups of three at each MWB around the classroom, puzzling over how to use their symbols, letters, numbers and words in a creative way to represent their tense under a time limit of fifteen or twenty minutes.

Assign the following roles: two scribes (who write/draw on the MWB – insist on a maximum of two marker pens allowed per group) and a dictionary and textbook researcher. If you need another role for a group of four then have a 'go to' student (to inspire the group and also to check whether the group is adhering to the number of symbols, letters, numbers and words allowed). The number of symbols, letters, numbers and words that can be used is at the teacher's discretion. This FLA assumes a limit of eight.

The FLA doesn't have to be completed on the MWB on the walls; it depends on the nature of the class. If you're worried about students 'stealing' each other's ideas, then it's probably better not to have their working visible. However, if the class responds to an environment in which they are inspired by other students, leave the MWB up. As you wander round the classroom you can get groups across the class to comment on and learn from other groups' ideas.

The first time I ran this FLA, one group represented the conjugation of the 'I' form with the following symbols: 👁4m = é. I had to ask them to explain. They said that they had used the eye symbol to represent the subject 'I'. The number 4 was a way of representing *for* with the *m* completing the word *form*, the equals sign was, well, just an equals sign, and finally they had used the *é* to represent the ending used to conjugate the preterite tense in the 'I' form for an *-ar* verb. This group had used two of their allotted symbols – the *eye* and the *equals sign*, one of their allotted numbers – the 4, and two of their allotted letters – the *m* and the *é*. All in all, a nice way of representing *the 'I' form equals é*.

This activity certainly gets the students thinking about how to form the tense.

Preparation and resources

- Identify the tense that you want the students to represent in groups. Type out the formation of the tense onto a PowerPoint slide.
- Stick up enough MWBs around your classroom so that there are enough for groups of four students (at most) to work at.
- Allot two marker pens for each group of students.
- Supply enough textbooks and other resources which have a reminder of the formation of the tense the groups will be representing.
- Arrange your classroom seating plan so that groups can work around a MWB.
- Project the formation of the tense onto the board so that all the students can see it.

Instructions

- Explain that the class will be working in groups of three (or four) at a MWB. Each group has to find a way of representing how to form a tense that has been recently covered. The group assigns the following roles: two scribes and one dictionary and textbook researcher.
- They may use up to eight symbols, letters, numbers and words to show how the tense is formed. Model how they could use some of these, as above.

- They have a twenty-minute time limit to produce this. Each group then has one minute to explain to the rest of the class their use of the symbols, letters, numbers and words and how these represent how the tense works.

Variations to the FLA

- Instead of the groups working on the same tense to represent, give the students a list of tenses from which to choose and let them represent that one.
- Vary the number of symbols, letters, numbers and words that the groups can use as a class or vary the number that individual groups can use within the class.
- Set a minimum number of symbols, letters, numbers and words that the groups have to use.
- Record each group's representation. Play the recording as the students are entering class the following lesson.

Teacher notes

So that students don't get bogged down in obsessing over the number of symbols used and thereby being distracted from the creative process of actually representing the tense, err on the side of caution with a slightly higher allocation of symbols, letters, numbers and words to use. It gives the students a little more leeway to be creative.

13 Boards, Bells and Textbook Tasks (FLA)

There's nothing like Boards, Bells and Textbook Tasks to liven up some textbook exercises. This FLA involves groups competing against each other to complete textbook tasks.

Make some PowerPoint slides each with a different textbook task on it. For French, all you need is *Exercice 4 Page 23*. Find about twelve or so exercises from the textbook on topics that have already been covered with the class, but which the students have not yet completed.

Get some bells! Sixteen hotel reception bells was one of my stranger purchases, but they're versatile and used judiciously add to the rapport with a class. These props might seem a poor teacher's substitute for *ActiVote* devices, but they certainly have their uses, especially with this FLA (and with Random VFLA #2).[15]

The students get into groups of three or four and are given a textbook, a dictionary, a bell, a marker pen, five counters and a MWB. The students take on the following roles: scribe (does the writing on the MWB), dictionary researcher (checks the dictionary) and textbook researcher (checks the textbook).

Groups complete an exercise from the textbook. Then they call you over to check that they are correct. How do they call you over? They ring the bell – once only. Any over-ringing gets punished by warnings and losing points.

---

[15] See www.prometheanworld.com/us/english/education/products/assessment-and-student-response/.

Once three groups have completed the task, don't wait for the other groups to catch up. Click on the next slide for the next exercise. Groups figure out what to do for the task and then do it. However, there is one more twist. The group may use one of their counters to get you, the teacher expert, to explain what they have to do. If a group chooses to spend a counter for an explanation, they must ring the bell and ask for help in the Target Language.

This FLA forces students to be more resilient. They have to deal with the dreaded 'I don't get it' curse by collaborating to work out what to do (decode the Target Language textbook instruction) or else forfeit a counter for your explanation. (Note: the textbook exercises that we've been using in recent years have the task instructions in the Target Language. It is good practice for students to get used to the new specification changes which have Target Language instructions on the GCSE exam papers.)

When all the exercises have been completed, the groups add the number of counters that they have left to their points won throughout the FLA; the winning group is the one with the most points.

Preparation and resources

- Get a bell, marker pen, MWB, textbook, dictionary and five counters for each group of three.
- Identify twelve exercises and their page references from the textbook (from modules already covered) that you want to use on the PowerPoint. Number each exercise and put each page reference on a separate slide.
- To avoid students cheating it's probably better not to stick the MWBs up on the walls. You don't want the distraction of students saying their work is being copied by another group.
- No specific seating plan is required for this FLA.
- Project the first exercise with the page reference on the board so that every student can see it.

Instructions

- Explain to the class that they are going to work in groups of three competing against other groups to complete exercises from the textbook.
- Each PowerPoint slide has a different exercise and its page reference from the textbook.
- Each group allocates the following roles: scribe, dictionary researcher and textbook researcher (as described above).
- Groups work together to complete the exercise. They then ring the bell to call you over to check it. The first three groups to do so correctly win a point. Once three groups have completed the exercise show the next slide and all groups start on the new task.

- The bell can only be used to call you over to check or for help. If they need help they must spend a counter for you to explain. Any help they need must be asked for in the Target Language.
- At the end of the twelve exercises, any counters a group has left will be converted into points and added to their total score.

Variations to the FLA

- Vary the number of textbook exercises.
- Vary how students can win a point. Award teacher discretionary points to groups who use consistently good Target Language; groups who are working well as a team; three points for the first group to complete the exercise correctly, two for the second group and one for the third.
- Offer groups the opportunity to sell a point or a counter for an extra resource such as another textbook or dictionary.
- Use fake Euros instead of counters. The students practise numbers by having to tell you the amount they will pay for an explanation in the Target Language.
- Instead of textbook tasks prepare grammar exercises to complete.
- Have two tasks from the textbook on each slide. The main task is worth a point and the subsidiary task half a point for those groups who finish first and second to complete, so that they have an extension exercise to do before you move on.

Teacher notes

Overzealous bell ringing is a temptation, and it's going to happen. If it affects the performance of this FLA then, if you have good rapport with the class, explain that over-ringing means they will lose points.

My preference is to use MWBs rather than exercise books or mini-whiteboards, simply because some textbook tasks might require answers that would not fit on mini-whiteboards. You may find it easier to check what's on the MWB from across the room if a group holds up its MWB.

If the same group is winning all the time then swap some students around with other groups.

This FLA is fast-paced and competitive. You will have students working together in a noisy, rapid-fire, pressurised environment, so make sure that there's not an assessment going on in the next room!

14 To The Walls (FLA)

To The Walls is an instant, group-based FLA mainly used for verb drills. It makes students' learning and the impact of your own feedback (when the students make alterations on the MWBs) immediately visible.

To The Walls utilises the 'classroom within a classroom'. Stick MWBs up around the room so that there are enough for groups of three to work at.

Identify the tense endings you want the students to practise, for example, the preterite tense in Spanish. Start by projecting the endings of the preterite tense for all subject pronouns onto the whiteboard at the front. Then reveal a list of regular Spanish infinitives with the English meaning next to each, so that students can see both the list of infinitives and the endings for forming the tense.

The students get into groups of three and stand by a MWB. The group assigns the following roles: scribe (writes on the MWB), checker (checks what the scribe has written) and tense endings boss (calls out each ending for the tense).

Call out one of the infinitives on the board. Each group works together to write the conjugation of the infinitive for each subject pronoun in the preterite tense. They also have to write the English meaning. For example, suppose you call out the infinitive, *hablar*.

Each group writes the following on their MWB:

> *hablé* = I spoke
> *hablaste* = you (singular) spoke
> etc.

The first group to write the whole paradigm wins a point. After calling out another infinitive from the list, circulate and give feedback on whether or not they have the correct endings.

Because there's more space on MWBs, students can fit more than one full paradigm on it. If students leave up their MWBs with examples of correct paradigms, these can be used as a model or reference for other students later in the lesson when they are doing some written work; for example, applying their knowledge of the tense to produce their own paragraph in their books.

This FLA is a good rapport builder and can be used whenever you feel the class needs a change in activity midway through a lesson. Just call out 'To The Walls', give an infinitive and the name of the tense you want the students to conjugate, and watch them get writing.

You can also start a lesson using this FLA. As soon as students enter the classroom, call out, 'Write five words that you learned last lesson on the walls, now! Do it! Go! Go! Go!' It's a good way of instantly demonstrating progress and also of practising retrieval. By leaving the MWBs up over time you can use the concept of spaced practice and get students to write what they learned two or three lessons ago. This is a good demonstration of making that learning visible.

Make it competitive. As the students come into class challenge them to write ten words from last week's topic with the English next to it on the MWBs as quickly as they can. The winner gets to keep the language trophy on their desk for the rest of the lesson.

Preparation and resources

- Identify the Target Language tense and the list of regular infinitives that you want to practise. Copy the tense endings and the list of regular infinitives onto a PowerPoint slide.
- Stick up enough MWBs around your classroom so that there are enough for groups of three to work at. Get a set of marker pens.
- Project the tense conjugation and list of regular infinitives onto the board so that every student can see them.

Instructions

- Explain to the class that they are going to work in groups of three on the MWBs to conjugate verbs.
- The students get into their groups, stand by a MWB and assign the roles of scribe, checker and tense endings boss (roles as described above). Give the scribe in each group a marker pen.
- Call out a Target Language infinitive from the list on the board. Each group works together to write the whole paradigm/verb pattern (or a term that the students are familiar with) of the infinitive together with the English.
- Model an example yourself on a group's MWB.
- The group to write the whole paradigm first wins a point. You will then call out another infinitive, and so on, until one group has scored five points.

Variations to the FLA

- Only project the list of infinitives to see if students can recall how to write whole paradigms without any support.
- Instead of verb endings get students to do the Verbal Volley (VFLA #8) on the MWBs. Project a list of vocabulary and have one student writing and speaking a Target Language word and English meaning, followed by the other student doing the same with the next word down the list and so on.
- Students swap their roles after every infinitive, so that the scribe gets to be the checker and so on.
- Run the FLA with pairs at each MWB. Give each student a marker pen. Student A can only write Target Language and B can only write the English for it.
- Use To The Walls for practising several tenses. Have the formation of three, four, five different tenses projected on the board with a set of regular infinitives. Call out the infinitive followed by the tense you want the students to conjugate. For example, 'Put *comer* in the present tense!' If the students know the Target Language for the names of the different tenses then use that.
- Incorporate your windows! Get some window pens and use your windows as additional boards on which the students can write (you could also use the windows as a makeshift display and write some key irregular verbs on them for students to refer to throughout the year).

Teacher notes

A quick extension task for students who have finished a writing task in their books is to get them to copy their examples onto a MWB, which you can then use as a model for other students. This makes students' progress immediate and visible.

15 Write, Pass, Read, Write, Pass (FLA)

This FLA works well for adding to and improving language. It uses picture cues to stimulate recall of relevant vocabulary. It's a good way of revising. The plan is to get the students to write down as much relevant vocabulary as possible.

For example, if you have covered the topic of Where I Live – from the type of house you live in, to aspects of the local region in terms of attractions and facilities – create a PowerPoint of five slides to cover the different aspects of this topic. Have one slide describing houses; one with Target Language terms about the town, the region, and so on. The tasks could be: 'Describe the type of house you live in', 'Say what there is in your town', 'Say what there is to visit in your region', 'Say where you visited in the past' and 'Say where you would like to visit in the future.'

Project the first slide and tell the students that they have two minutes to write all that they can in the Target Language on a piece of paper. At the end of two minutes they pass the paper to the student to their right. They now have two minutes to read the work they have been given, and then add to and/or correct the work.

Once the two minutes are up, students pass the work on to the student on their right again. They spend the next two minutes reading, adding to or correcting what they have received.

After two turns of adding and correcting show the second slide: 'Say what there is in your town'. Students write on the paper they now have (not on the paper they had initially). After two minutes they pass the paper to the student to their right and the process continues until all the tasks have been completed.

How much support you give depends on how much language the students can recall spontaneously. You might want them to have a copy of the textbook or a handout of some key vocab and phrases.

It's a good idea to have modelled specific techniques that students could use in order to improve the quality of their language during the two-minute adding and correcting stage. For example, using adjectives with nouns, using conjunctions such as *cuando/où/weil*.

Once all the tasks have been completed, either take the papers in to mark or make what has been produced more visible to the students for instant feedback. When visualisers were popular in the classroom I used one to project and comment on the language produced in this FLA so that any mistakes could be ironed out straight away.

Preparation and resources

- Identify the topic that you want to get students writing about and create five Target Language tasks for each topic on separate PowerPoint slides.
- Either stick up MWBs around your classroom so that there are enough for a dozen or so examples of the completed tasks to be written up, or set up a visualiser or a digital camera to allow you to give feedback on the completed tasks.
- Give each student a piece of lined paper. Allow students access to a dictionary and a relevant double page spread of vocabulary in the textbook.
- Set up a timing device so that the students can see how long they have left.
- Arrange your classroom seating plan so that you can divide the class into halves.
- Project the first Target Language task onto the board so that every student can see it.

Instructions

- Explain that they have two minutes to write down what they know of the topic on the lined paper to answer the Target Language task on the board.
- After two minutes, every student passes their paper to the student on their right. (The student at the end of the line completes the loop by passing their paper to the student who has no one to their left.)
- Once they have their classmate's written piece they have another two minutes to correct and/or add to what is on the paper.

- After another two minutes they again pass the paper to the student to their right, and spend another two minutes correcting and/or adding to what is on the paper.
- Then show the next Target Language task.
- The process repeats, with students using the piece of paper they now have.
- After five tasks, collect the papers in and give feedback on the language used.

Variations to the FLA

- Vary the time for writing and checking.
- Instead of tasks to write about make some sentences to translate into the Target Language with students checking and elaborating on the translation when the translation is passed on.
- At a higher level give the students longer than two minutes to write a mini-essay paragraph before passing on the paper.
- Get the students to speak what they have written before passing the paper and the students receiving the paper then say what's written on the paper.
- Use different coloured pens for the students adding or correcting.

Teacher notes

With this FLA a lot depends on students' prior knowledge. They need to have a thorough grounding in the topic so that they can write about it and be in a position to constructively criticise what another student has written.

This FLA can be the basis of a whole lesson, especially when feeding back to the class on what has been written.

16 Digital Feedback (FLA)

This FLA has students listening to a recording of you feeding back on one of their classmate's written pieces. There's more to it than just listening, though; students need to understand what you say and mark the piece themselves exactly as you would have marked it. They themselves write on their classmates' books.

It is vital to provide feedback which the students can hear, use and understand. In the introduction to *How to Give Effective Feedback to Your Students*, Brookhart writes that students cannot hear something if they are not listening to it.[16] That sounds obvious, but it's often the case that people need to learn how to receive feedback – for a start, they need to have a growth mindset and be open to learning.[17] This is the philosophical basis of the Digital Feedback FLA. Students must listen in order to correct other students' mistakes.

Once the student has heard your commentary and marked another student's book, the owner of the book reads their marked work and uses a purple pen to annotate it. Why a purple pen? That's my preference; other colours are available! Actually, there is a fair bit out there about using purple pens, including a mention in a 2014 Ofsted report,[18] and their use alongside Dedicated Improvement and Reflection Time (DIRT).

---

[16] S. M. Brookhart, (2008) *How to Give Effective Feedback to Your Students*, Association for Supervision & Curriculum Development. p. 2.

[17] C. S. Dweck, (2012) *Mindset: How You Can Fulfil Your Potential*, London, Constable & Robinson.

[18] Ofsted, (2014) *Inspection Report: Fernhill School*, 20–21 March. p. 5. See http://www.ofsted.gov.uk/inspection-reports/find-inspection-report/provider/ELS/116447.

You take the books in but instead of writing your feedback and corrections, you make an audio recording in the form of a commentary. There are several ways of recording yourself:

- You could make a podcast.
- You could use Vocaroo (http://vocaroo.com/). This is a simple tool for creating an audio file; you can email it out very quickly.
- You could use Audacity (http://audacity.sourceforge.net/).
- On Joe Dale's blog, 'Integrating ICT into the MFL classroom', he refers to using Google Talk as a tool for providing audio feedback. (See http://joedale.typepad.com/integrating_ict_into_the_/2009/05/using-google-talk-for-audio-feedback.html.)

Despite all these digital solutions, I'm actually quite dull and traditional when recording commentaries for this FLA: I use a digital Dictaphone (hence the name of this FLA). I record a separate sound file for each student which I then email out, put on the school's shared area or make accessible on the school's Virtual Learning Environment (VLE).

The objective is to give a fellow student precise feedback on what is wrong with the paragraph and what they need to do to correct it. You're not just pointing out the mistakes in the piece, but telling the student who is listening what is wrong, why it is wrong, and what to do to change it.

Here is a short sample introduction:

Tom has used the 'I' form, the 'we' form and the 'they' form of the present tense brilliantly here so write this down please. Circle the following examples of this in his writing; when Tom uses x, y and z. He needs to correct the following nouns so please circle the following words and write 'SP' next to each so that Tom will know to look these up in the dictionary and rewrite these correctly. These nouns are […]. Please write a comment that says that Tom should write these nouns correctly three times each with the English meaning next to each word.

Finish the commentary by giving the student who is listening and marking it a choice of possible questions that they can add for the student to answer when they get their book back. For example, you could say something like:

Choose one of the three questions I'm going to say and it write it down underneath the piece of work. Write 'Tom, please answer this.' The first question you can choose is 'Can you explain why you have used this time phrase with this tense?' If you choose this question, you need to draw an arrow to the first sentence in the first line of the piece. The second question you could choose is 'Can you give some examples of the adjectives that you could use with these nouns here?' and circle the nouns vacances *and* hôtel. *The third question is …*

By offering a choice of questions you are getting the student who is listening to actively engage with the process of marking the piece and to think for themselves about which would be the most appropriate question to add, based on what they have heard and marked so far. This is more than you just telling them exactly what to do. Not only that, but by getting a student to write a question down you are encouraging a questioning and learning dialogue between student and student in their books.

With this FLA you are also modelling how you would feed back to a student. Essentially you are helping to train students in more effective peer assessment, practising giving feedback effectively.

Preparation and resources

- Choose a topic for which you want to set the students written homework; for example, writing about holidays they have been on.
- Prepare a way of recording the feedback commentary as described above – and get some purple pens!
- This FLA takes place over four lessons. In lesson one, set the homework task; lesson two, take in students' books and then record the commentary feedback; lesson three, give the books to different students to write your comments in; and lesson four, give the students their own books back to annotate the comments with purple pens of progress.

Instructions

- Set the written homework piece in lesson one. Tell the students that you are not going to write anything on their piece when they hand it in; instead, you will record a feedback commentary.
- After students hand in their homework at the end of lesson two, you will record a separate sound file for each student, giving specific feedback.
- Towards the end of lesson three get two students to hand out the books so that each student receives somebody else's book. Make a list of who gets which other student's work.
- Explain how they are to listen to your recorded commentary on the written homework piece. (Distribute the sound files as described above: by email, on the school's VLE, etc.)
- When listening to the recorded commentary, students must actually write the corrections and positive feedback comments in the student's book according to how you have spoken (as in the example above).
- They should use a different coloured pen from the one used by the student who wrote the paragraph, but not purple. They must bring the book they have marked to the next lesson.

- At the start of lesson four the students give the books back to their owners. Give out the purple pens and ask the students to read the comments.
- Tell the students to respond accordingly to the feedback in their book using the purple pens. Finally, get the students to feed back to you on how this FLA has gone.

Variations to the FLA

- Instead of getting the students to write the feedback commentary for homework, book a computer room (or language lab) where students listen to the feedback and then write down what they hear. The next stage – returning the books – can begin in the same lesson.
- Instead of making an audio file commentary make a video instead. You could use Moodle (although this requires technical savvy).[19]

Teacher notes

Make sure that there is enough time between lessons three and four for students to access the sound file, listen to the audio commentary and write the comments. Offer options on how to access the sound file if recording each commentary with a digital Dictaphone.

After giving this feedback there's more feedback that could be done. Get the students to feed back on your feedback. Hattie says that expert teachers should look for feedback and adapt their own teaching as this impacts on students' learning.[20]

When you record your commentary withhold the actual marks that you would give the pieces. Only pass these on to students after the feedback processes have taken place.

---

[19] See http://www.moodlenews.com/2011/adding-video-feedback-to-the-assignment-activity/.

[20] Hattie, (2012) p. 29.

17 Back To Front (FLA)

This translation activity could almost be a VFLA. In Back To Front, the students work in pairs: the student facing the board calls out a sentence in the Target Language, and their partner, who is facing away, translates it into English. Use material that the students have covered recently as this FLA is a competitive way of testing retrieval of vocabulary and longer phrases.

Project a set of Target Language phrases and sentences, together with the English translation, in different text boxes on the board, as in the following example. The numbers in brackets on the slide are the points value for each phrase. The longer, more complicated phrases or sentences score a higher number of points.

les maths = maths (1)	*Quelle est ta matière préférée?* = What is your favourite subject? (2)
la technologie = DT (1)	*J'adore l'anglais parce que c'est génial.* = I like English because it's great. (2)
l'informatique = ICT (1)	*Je n'aime pas le dessin car le prof est ennuyeux.* = I don't like art because the teacher is boring. (2)
l'EPS = PE (1)	*J'adore l'EPS parce que le prof est cool.* = I love PE because the teacher is cool. (2)
le théâtre = drama (1)	*le français* = French (1)
la musique = music (1)	*Ma matière préférée c'est ...* = My favourite school subject is ... (2)

The student looking at the board calls out the Target Language for one of the phrases or sentences. Their partner, who cannot see the board, calls out the English. If this student translates the sentence correctly they both turn to face the opposite direction. Each student keeps a tally of the number of points that they have won for getting the translation correct.

This process repeats. For every correct answer the pair turns around. This alternation only stops if the student with their back to the board cannot translate the phrase correctly. If that happens, the student facing the board calls out a different phrase, and keeps trying different phrases until their partner does translate it correctly. There is also a time limit on this FLA so pairs must aim to score as many points as possible within their allotted time.

This FLA is not about competing within pairs, but about pairs working together to compete to get the most points. Students' recall is being tested continually and rewarded instantly. It is a fast-paced paired activity which you can observe working at its best when you see a pair of students consistently twisting and turning, speaking and translating in their seats.

Preparation and resources

- Identify the topic that you want students to practise; for example, School Subjects, as in the example on page 154.
- Choose a dozen or so phrases and vocabulary from the topic and type the Target Language and English translation into text boxes on a PowerPoint slide.
- For vocabulary items put a 1 in brackets after the word and for longer phrases put a 2 in brackets, as illustrated in the example on page 154.
- Project the language slide onto the board.

Instructions

- The students work in pairs with one student looking at the vocabulary and phrases on the board and the other student turning away. Set a five- or ten-minute time limit.
- The student looking at the board starts by speaking just the Target Language for one of the phrases or vocabulary items on the board; the student turned away says the English for it.
- If the student translates the phrase or vocabulary correctly they score the appropriate number of points. They then turn to face the board while their partner turns to face away.
- The student now looking at the board calls out the Target Language for a different phrase or vocabulary for their partner to translate.
- For every correct response they both turn to face the opposite direction.

- This process continues until a student does not translate the word or phrase correctly or does not know the translation. When this happens the other student calls out a different word or phrase.
- Once a Target Language phrase or vocabulary has been used, neither student can say it again until another five have been tried.
- At the end of the time limit the pair with the most points wins.

Variations to the FLA

- One student says the English for the phrases and vocabulary and the student turned away gives the Target Language. Students get double points awarded for this.
- Mix up the practice: leave it to the students' discretion whether to say the English or the Target Language.
- Prepare three slides with language from different topics to use for revision. Spend five minutes on each slide. Students total their score for all three.
- As with Bob-Up Classic (VFLA #1), test retrieval by asking the students to write their own list of vocabulary or phrases they have learned in the lesson, then project this list onto the board for Back To Front in the following lesson.
- The students compete against each other within the pair; if the student gets a translation correct they win the points for themselves. The student with the most points at the end wins.

Teacher notes

Students do not need to actually have their backs to the board. They can just turn their head away to make it easier to turn back and forth.

18 Pull The Switch (FLA)

This FLA is a confidence booster for speaking. Students have the opportunity to practise speaking a dialogue in the Target Language in pairs (as Student A and Student B). Then you 'Pull The Switch', whereupon they only have access to the English transcript. The aim is to have students speaking the dialogue without having to refer to the Target Language script at all. A further aim is to have students speaking the dialogue without any prompts, and showing a measure of spontaneity by substituting nouns or opinion phrases in the dialogue.

Prepare a document where the first half contains a dialogue that includes at least four utterances for both A and B in the Target Language (see the following example). The second half of the document has the English translations.

A: *Est-ce que tu aimes le français?*
B: *Oui, j'aime le français parce que c'est génial.*
A: *Est-ce que tu aimes l'anglais?*
B: *Non, je n'aime pas l'anglais parce que c'est ennuyeux.*
A: *Est-ce que tu aimes l'informatique?*
B: *Oui, j'adore l'informatique parce que c'est intéressant. Et toi?*
A: *Non, je n'aime pas l'informatique parce que je n'aime pas le prof. Est-ce que tu aimes le dessin?*
B: *Oui, j'adore le dessin parce que le prof est génial.*

Project both parts of the dialogue on the board. Model the dialogue by speaking it with a student in front of the class. Give each pair a handout with the same dialogue. The students, as A and B, run through the Target Language dialogue. Set a time limit for this.

Then tell the students to fold their handouts over so that they can only see the English and not the Target Language. They now have another five minutes to speak their dialogue in the Target Language but only looking at the English. They are allowed to look back at the Target Language version, but lose a point if they do. This makes the FLA competitive: at the end of the five minutes the pair losing the fewest combined total points wins.

Preparation and resources

- Identify the topic and language you want to practise as a dialogue. For example, a list of questions and answers to do with School Subjects, as in the example on page 157.
- Divide the dialogue into A and B utterances. Copy the dialogue onto the first half of a PowerPoint slide and copy the English translation of the dialogue below it.
- Prepare a class set of handouts with the Target Language dialogue on the top half and the English below, for the students to have one each.
- Project the handout onto the board so that every student can see it.

Instructions

- Give the dialogue handout to each student. The students work in pairs as A and B, and read just the Target Language dialogue.
- They spend ten minutes reading this dialogue through several times.
- Pull The Switch. The students fold the handout so that they can only see the English version of the dialogue. Turn off the projected handout on the board.
- They then spend five minutes speaking the Target Language dialogue but only looking at the English translation.
- If students get stuck and can't remember what to say they may remind themselves by glancing at the Target Language half of the dialogue. However, every time they look back they lose a point.
- At the end of the five minutes the winning pair is the one with fewest points lost.

Variations to the FLA

- Vary the time allowed before Pulling The Switch. Have a different time limit for different pairs; more confident pairs have less time to practise the Target Language dialogue before switching.

- Following some concise modelling, get the students to produce their own dialogues to use by another pair in the class. Once checked for accuracy by you, the pairs select another pair to give the dialogue to, who then have to translate it into English before running the FLA as above.
- Instead of a dialogue, project a list of key vocabulary and run the FLA as a VFLA. Students work in pairs writing down three different Target Language words for every utterance in the 'dialogue' with the English meanings of the words underneath.
- Instead of a question and answer dialogue have a list of opinions to practise.

Teacher notes

Monitor how well the students are adapting to the task by observing how often they need to refer to the support. Clearly, if students constantly need prompts then they should have further time for practising just reading the Target Language dialogue.

Students need a fair amount of positive reinforcement with this FLA since they are being persistently reminded of what they do and don't know. If pairs are struggling after you have pulled the switch give them more time speaking just the Target Language dialogue until they have the confidence to switch.

19 Project A Board Game (FLA)

This FLA is a Target Language testing game based on the traditional board game of Snakes and Ladders. The students play Snakes and Ladders according to the usual rules of the game with the difference that each time they land on a numbered square they have to say a Target Language word and the English translation.

The board is multi-functional, in that it has only numbered squares and Snakes and Ladders symbols. The squares are left blank. The content comes separately, consisting of whatever you want the students to practise, laid out in the same grid pattern as the board (see the example on page 161).

In addition, this content is also projected as a PowerPoint slide on the whiteboard at the front of the class. Provide a half-class set of handouts with the translation for the content that is projected on the board in the same grid pattern. The students play the game, landing on numbered squares on the laminated board, and then find the specific content on the accompanying handout.

The students work in pairs, each with a Snakes and Ladders laminate and a handout with the vocabulary in front of them.

Suppose that a student starts by throwing a four. They move their counter on the laminate, then find the corresponding square on their handout or on the image projected on the board.

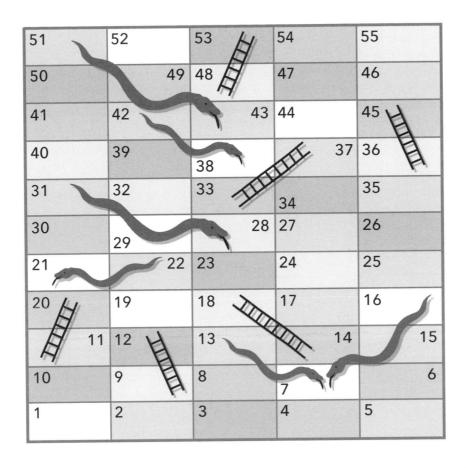

51	52	53	54	55
50	49	48	47	46
41	42	43	44	45
40	39	38	37	36
31	32	33	34	35
30	29	28	27	26
21	22	23	24	25
20	19	18	17	16
11	12	13	14	15
10	9	8	7	6
1	2	3	4	5

51. *Informatik*	52. *Kunst*	53. *Mathe*	54. *Musik*	55. *schwer*
50. *Geschichte*	49. *Französisch*	48. *Erdkunde*	47. *Englisch*	46. *Deutsch*
41. *leicht*	42. *schwer*	43. *Biologie*	44. *Chemie*	45. *Theater*
40. *interessant*	39. *nützlich*	38. *Wirtschaft*	37. *Sport*	36. *Spanisch*
31. *Kunst*	32. *Mathe*	33. *Musik*	34. *Physik*	35. *Religion*
30. *Informatik*	29. *Geschichte*	28. *Französisch*	27. *Erdkunde*	26. *Englisch*
21. *schwer*	22. *Biologie*	23. *Chemie*	24. *Theater*	25. *Deutsch*
20. *leicht*	19. *interessant*	18. *nützlich*	17. *Wirtschaft*	16. *Sport*
11. *Mathe*	12. *Musik*	13. *Physik*	14. *Religion*	15. *Spanisch*
10. *Kunst*	9. *Informatik*	8. *Geschichte*	7. *Französisch*	6. *Erdkunde*
1. *Biologie*	2. *Chemie*	3. *Theater*	4. *Deutsch*	5. *Englisch*

They see that number four is *Deutsch,* and say, '*Deutsch,* German!' If their partner decides that their translation is correct the student leaves their counter on number four and the turn passes to their partner. If the student doesn't know the translation or gets the translation wrong they move their counter back one place and the turn then passes to their partner.

The student who is listening to their partner's translation can assess whether their partner's translation is correct by referring to a translation handout.

The board game format does require a bit of initial resource-making, but once you have a set of laminates you can easily adapt the content of the slide you project to suit any topic you wish.

Preparation and resources

- Identify the topic and the Target Language you want to practise with a class, such as School Subjects.
- To make a Snakes and Ladders game board create a table on a PowerPoint slide (five columns and eleven rows), number each box, add the snakes and ladders icons, copy the document onto A3 and laminate it. Make enough copies for a half-class set.
- Type the Target Language that you want the students to be speaking using the same table layout with the numbered squares, but without the snakes and ladders symbols.
- Get some dice, counters, and make a half-class set of handouts which have the translations for the Target Language you are projecting on the whiteboard.
- Project the Target Language table onto the board so that every student can see it.

Instructions

- Explain to the class that they are going to use a board game for practising the language shown in the table on the projected slide.
- Hand out the Snakes and Ladders laminates, dice, counters and translation handout to each pair of students.
- The students work in pairs. One student rolls the die and moves their counter that number of spaces on the Snakes and Ladders board. They then look up to find the corresponding Target Language word in the same numbered box on the projected slide.
- The student then speaks the Target Language and the translation for that word.
- Their partner checks the translation. If it is correct the student leaves their counter where it landed. If not, they move it back one space.
- This FLA continues with students taking turns following the usual rules of Snakes and Ladders until one student wins by reaching the last square.

Variations to the FLA

- Vary the content of the text boxes: use phrases, short sentences or irregular verbs.
- Instead of Target Language in the text boxes use English.

Teacher notes

Once you have a set of game board templates you can make a board game out of most language.

Use other board designs to play on. For example, place text boxes around an image of a football pitch, a map of a town, a map of a street, a plan of a shopping centre, or a track leading up and down a mountain and so on. As long as the boxes on the laminates are left blank and are numbered then you can create a board game with any content you choose.

20 Walkie-Talkies (FLA)

This FLA forces students to communicate in groups. The students get practice in their spoken Target Language, both in their ability to correctly transcribe a passage in the Target Language dictated to them by one of their colleagues, and in being able to ask questions about the process. This is a lesson-long FLA.

Having been given some walkie-talkies as a present, I wondered how I could use them in the classroom context. One of the features of the walkie-talkie is that it involves communicating with another person without seeing their body language. My logic ran thus: if students use a walkie-talkie to communicate and are unable to see each other, then listening becomes all important.

I prepared two short Target Language paragraphs of similar length and difficulty on the topic that the students had just been learning about (Home Town and Region) and copied each paragraph onto a separate piece of paper.

(I bought another set of walkie-talkies so the description of this FLA involves two sets, but you could use just one set and run the FLA with the whole class.)

Two students stand at the front of the class, each with a walkie-talkie, facing their side of the class. Ask for one volunteer from each side of the class, and give these students the matching walkie-talkies, so that they can communicate with their partner standing at the front. Also give these students a copy of the Target Language paragraphs. They go outside the classroom, and using the walkie-talkie, read out their paragraph to their partner inside the classroom. The partner listens, and clarifies any words or phrases by asking the speaker to repeat, speak more clearly, spell, slow down, and so on. All communication requests must be made in the Target Language. So that they know how to make such requests, before doing this FLA, drill into the students command phrases such as 'Please repeat the sentence' or 'Could you spell out that word' in the Target Language. The success of the FLA depends on students' prior knowledge of these key Target Language instructions.

To give the rest of the class something to do while the two students are communicating with each other, ask the listening partner to repeat out loud what they have heard; the rest of the class writes this down. The students in the classroom may also use the Target Language commands and requests with the student facing them, asking them to slow down, repeat, spell words and so on.

Once all the students on a side of the class have written their dictated paragraph, the student who has been outside comes in and, together with their walkie-talkie partner, gives all the students on their side a handout of the paragraph that they have been using, and the students mark their own work, giving themselves a mark for every word they have spelled correctly. The student(s) in the class with the highest number of words spelled correctly wins.

The key idea behind this is that there is a lot of communication going on where students must use the Target Language and rely on each other to achieve their goal of spelling the paragraph accurately.

Just make sure the walkie-talkies are charged up.

Preparation and resources

- Get a set (two sets if possible) of walkie-talkies.
- Identify the topic that you want to practise with the students. Write two different paragraphs on the topic which are the same in length and similar in their perceived difficulty level. Copy each paragraph onto a separate document and make enough copies of each paragraph for the students on each side of the class.
- Arrange your classroom seating plan so that you can divide the class into two.
- Set up the projector so that you just have to click to reveal the paragraphs.

Instructions

- Explain that this is a lesson-long FLA which involves a lot of Target Language communicative phrases (ones that they have learned prior to this lesson).
- Ask for four volunteers: two students from each side.

- Explain that you will send out one student from each side; the other two students will stay in class and face their own side.
- The students who go outside are given a Target Language paragraph and a walkie-talkie. The matching walkie-talkie is given to their partner, who remains in the classroom.
- The students outside speak their paragraph to their partners inside using the walkie-talkie. The student inside repeats what they hear to the students who face them, who then copy down what is said to them in the Target Language.
- The rule is that all communication, including asking the students to slow down, speak more clearly, repeat what has been said, spell words, and so on, must be done in the Target Language. The paragraphs may be spoken as many times as the students want, provided that they ask for this in the Target Language.
- Once all of the students on a side have the paragraph copied down, give them each a handout with the correct version so they can mark their work. A word has to be spelled perfectly to get a mark. The student with the most points wins.

Variations to the FLA

- Instead of paragraphs being spoken, prepare a list of words or short sentences for the students to translate through the walkie-talkies.
- If you're able to borrow four iPads you could set up a Skype account and instead of walkie-talkies give the students who stand outside an iPad each; they can then dictate their paragraphs using Skype to the two students in class, who also have an iPad each. It would be better to have the students in class using headphones with the iPads so that the language that is spoken to them is not audible to the others.

Teacher notes

There are several layers of communication in this FLA. Students must use Target Language to communicate requests. If they don't use it, and start lapsing into English, then warnings and three-second time penalties should ensue where students must cease communication for a brief moment before they can continue.

When the students in class are correcting their paragraphs the students who were operating the walkie-talkies need a different task to complete. They could either support the students on their side by monitoring their marking or they could be given an extension task, such as translating the paragraph into English or translating the other team's paragraph.

You could extend this FLA into another lesson by running the Relay (FLA #3) with the texts in the follow-up lesson.

21 PronunciRace (FLA)

This FLA is concerned with students acquiring correct pronunciation of words in the Target Language. It is competitive and designed to celebrate accurate pronunciation of words.

In *Debates in Modern Languages Education*, Robert Woore refers to a study carried out by Lynn Erler which found that learners of French who lacked the ability to pronounce written words accurately were 'bound to take offence and become disaffected learners'. I've seen this myself in classrooms: a student mispronounces a word, another student laughs and the first student becomes demotivated. Even when I've given kind, corrective feedback on a student's pronunciation their perception has been that they can't do languages. Of course, much depends on *how* you correct the student's pronunciation. Using careful praise may avoid these potentially demotivating scenarios. Woore also refers to a further study carried out by Erler and Macaro (2011) which found that students in KS3 with better developed phonological decoding were more motivated to continue learning French after KS3.[21]

Correct pronunciation in the classroom is vital. Laughing at another student's inability to pronounce a word correctly is a put-down and must not be tolerated. Being surrounded by classmates who seem to be able to speak correctly draws attention to a student's shortfall and they could become embarrassed and demotivated. This is where the student's mindset is important. Do they see criticism or feedback as an attack on their identity, or is it a further opportunity to work harder and develop a better accent? This certainly matters when you find

---

[21] R. Woore in Driscoll et al., (2014) p. 91.

yourself actually immersed in the Target Language culture surrounded by native speakers. It takes a certain amount of resilience to withstand that.

This FLA relies very much on creating a supportive relationship not just between teacher and student but also between student and student; therefore I would not recommend trying this FLA with a new class. However, it works well once you have built a good, supportive rapport with a class.

Project a list of semi-familiar words on the board, much as you would do with the VFLAs, or you could try new vocabulary and rely on the students' ability to decode the orthography. Remember that most foreign languages have phonemes that don't exist in English (such as the rolling *r* and guttural consonants), and it may be difficult for some native English speakers to achieve perfect pronunciation.

Whatever you project, as with the VFLAs, one student begins by saying the first Target Language word and its English meaning. If their pronunciation of the word is accurate they continue down the list, speaking the next Target Language word and English. However, if another student believes that they have mispronounced a word then they make a challenge by raising their hand. You ask them to demonstrate how they think the word should be pronounced. If the challenger makes a correct challenge and pronounces the word correctly themselves they then take over pronouncing words on the list from where the last student left off.

If a student mispronounces a word and no other student challenges then you step in, pause the process, and model the correct pronunciation with the student and class who then all repeat the word correctly before continuing down the list.

Only students who make a correct challenge may take over. Even if a student makes a correct challenge on the last word and finishes the list they become PronunciRace Champion.

You might think it demotivating for those students who keep receiving challenges, but as long as they are given genuine praise, encouragement and – just as importantly – reminded of the correct pronunciation, then the classroom climate of support and positive reinforcement should not be affected. However, students must use the feedback immediately, and pronounce the word correctly.[22]

Preparation and resources

- Identify the group of Target Language words or phrases that you want for pronunciation practice. Copy the vocabulary or phrases onto a PowerPoint slide and number each item.

---

[22] See *Rule 23*, Lemov, (2012) p. 109.

- Project the vocabulary or phrases onto the board so that every student can see them.

Instructions

- Tell the students that you need a volunteer to start the PronunciRace FLA. This student starts by speaking the first Target Language word and English meaning on the projected list on the board.
- If any student thinks that that student has not pronounced a word correctly they can challenge by raising their hand. They will need to explain their challenge and pronounce the word how they think it should be said.
- If the challenge is correct, that student takes over reading the vocabulary list from where the previous student left off.
- If the challenge is incorrect you model the correct pronunciation and get the student who made the incorrect challenge to repeat it. The FLA continues with the student 'in play' speaking the next word down.
- If the student pronounces a word incorrectly but there is no challenge then you must intervene and model the correct pronunciation. The student must pronounce it correctly before continuing.
- A challenge can be made at any time but only after a correct challenge does the turn pass to a different student.
- The student who correctly speaks the last word on the list becomes PronunciRace Champion, regardless of how many previous words they have pronounced.

Variations to the FLA

- Have phrases or sentences rather than words.
- Run the FLA in groups led by a more phonologically confident student; they will act as the teacher-student, monitoring the rest of the group's pronunciation and debating the challenges accordingly. You would need to be very sure that the students had secure enough knowledge of correct pronunciation to do this.

Teacher notes

Hand a soft toy to the speaker, who passes it on to the student who makes a correct challenge.

22 Consequences (FLA)

This FLA is based on a traditional format, with a few minor tweaks. It requires students to create reasonably original responses to the prompts and can be used as a whole-lesson FLA.

Prepare six numbered Target Language tasks (with each task on a separate PowerPoint slide) about a topic that has recently been covered. For example, the English for each Target Language statement could be based on the topic of Holidays like this:

Slide 1. Say where you normally go on holiday and why.

Slide 2. Say where you went last year and how you got there.

Slide 3. Say who you went with last year and where you stayed.

Slide 4. Say where you are going to go next year and how you are going to get there.

Slide 5. Say who you are going to go with next year and where you are going to stay.

Slide 6. Say where you would like to go on holiday if you were to win the lottery.

The students in groups of three assign the following roles: scribe (does the writing), textbook researcher (accesses the double-page spread of vocabulary in the textbook) and dictionary researcher (checks and looks things up in the dictionary). Each group has a piece of lined paper upon which the group spends three minutes writing as much as they can in the Target Language to complete the first task on the board. They can use the textbook and dictionary to support them.

At the end of three minutes each group in the class folds the lined paper to hide what they have just written – as would be customary when playing Consequences at a party. They leave the paper on their desk and then move one place clockwise to another base.

Project slide two onto the board and each group answers this second question by writing as much as they can in three minutes. They write on the paper immediately below the folded bit. The groups may not unfold the paper to see what was written before. After three minutes they fold the paper to hide their input, leave it on the desk and move one place on. This continues until all six tasks have been completed. Then one member of each group brings you the folded paper for you to unfold and discuss.

Using a visualiser makes the discussion and feedback on Consequences much easier. Otherwise, lacking a means of giving instant feedback, you could slowly read out the unfolded pieces three times, asking the class to listen for any mistakes.

Preparation and resources

- Identify the topic you want the students writing about and type out six Target Language tasks to do with that topic, each on a separate PowerPoint slide.
- Provide lined paper for groups of three students. Allow all students access to a dictionary and relevant double-page spread of vocabulary in the textbook.
- Set up a timer so the students know how long they have left.
- Arrange your classroom seating plan so that it allows for groups of three to move around easily.
- Project the first Target Language task onto the board so that every student can see it.

Instructions

- Ask the students to get into groups of three, find a base, and assign the roles of scribe, textbook researcher and dictionary researcher.
- Hand out a piece of lined paper, a dictionary and a textbook to each group.
- Explain that each group has three minutes to write as much as they can to complete the first task on the board. They should use the textbook, the dictionary, their class notes and prior knowledge.

171

- After three minutes, each group folds the paper over to hide what they have just written. They leave the paper there and then move in a clockwise direction to the next base.
- Each group now has three minutes to write as much as they can to answer the second Target Language task. They write their response on the paper they find at the new base.
- This process continues until they have written answers to all six tasks on the board.
- Once the final task has been completed one student from each group brings you the paper. Unfold the sheet and provide feedback to the class on each piece.

Variations to the FLA

- Vary the time limit before each group moves.
- Be more true to the spirit of Consequences: instead of Target Language tasks project a short series of Target Language paragraphs, one per slide. The students then draw cartoons/pictures to illustrate what they understand by each paragraph. They fold the paper to hide each cartoon or picture, and do the same with the next paragraph. In this way, the students produce their own storyboard.
- Vary the tasks within the six that you project: have a couple of tasks as described above, a couple of sentences to translate and a couple of pictures to describe.
- If creating pictures is too artistically demanding for the students then project a short sentence on each slide for the groups to embellish using their prior knowledge of how to improve the quality of written pieces (see Progress Gallery FLA #39).
- Prepare and project some tasks from the textbook. Once completed, unfold them and get the groups to mark them.

Teacher notes

Play some appropriate music to do with the topic while the students are writing. Stop the music when the three-minute time limit is up.

Practically speaking, if you know your group writes a lot then you might want to prepare A3-sized pieces of lined paper for them to use.

23 Group Splat (FLA)

Splat is another regular in the language teacher's locker. This FLA adapts a popular traditional technique to allow more students to practise language simultaneously. If you're not familiar with Splat, then it usually goes something like this: you project ten or so images onto the board and ask two student volunteers to stand facing the board. You call out a Target Language word that refers to one of the images, and the first student to *tap* the correct image wins the point. (Taking the display system into consideration, a tap may be more appropriate than a full-force splat!)

Let's say that you are practising the words for fruit in a French lesson. You project ten or so images of different fruits onto the board. One of those images is of a strawberry. Call out the word *fraise* and the first student to tap the correct image is the winner. Repeat with *banane*, and so on. Once a student has three points they retire and another student takes over.

Of course this isn't the only way to do it. Other variations of Splat include:

- Projecting some Target Language words (not in a neat list but spread across the board) and calling out a word in English for the quicker student to splat.
- Projecting some English words and calling out the Target Language.
- Projecting images with the Target Language underneath.

Having experienced Splat as both student and teacher I've always found it an entertaining way to practise language. However, something I could never reconcile as a teacher when doing the activity was the niggling feeling of 'what are the other students in the class doing while these two students and I are running Splat?'.

Using the classroom within a classroom idea, groups of students could replicate what I was doing at MWBs around the room. However, unable to replicate ten projectors around the classroom for the students to project the images, I had to compromise. So, Group Splat runs like this: stick ten or so MWBs on the walls around the classroom with students working in groups of three by each one; one is the teacher-student and the other two are, well, students. Give each teacher-student a handout of the Target Language words projected on the board but with the English meanings. This enables them to check the correct translation for the words that the students in their group will be splatting.

Each group uses a marker pen to copy the Target Language phrases from the board at the front onto their own MWB. Now the students run Splat in their groups. The teacher-student calls out a Target Language word that is on their MWB and the two students try to be the first to splat the word and then call out the English for it. The teacher-student keeps track of points scored.

Groups of students practising Splat at MWBs around the room makes Group Splat …

Preparation and resources

- Identify the group of Target Language words or phrases that you want the groups to copy and splat on the MWBs. Arrange these all over a PowerPoint slide so that this is not just a list of vocabulary.
- Stick up MWBs around your classroom so that there are enough for groups of three students. Get a set of marker pens.
- Arrange your classroom to ensure students have enough space around their MWB.
- Project the vocabulary or phrases onto the board so that every student can see them.

Instructions

- Tell the class to get into groups of three and stand by a MWB.
- Give the class five seconds to decide who in their group will be the teacher-student. Give each teacher-student a marker pen and a copy of the Target Language words and English meanings as projected on the board.
- Each teacher-student should copy the Target Language onto their MWB.
- Each group runs Splat at their MWB the way it usually runs at the front. The other two students face the MWB, and the teacher-student calls out a Target Language word. The

quicker of the two students to splat the word and say the correct English translation wins a point. The teacher-student records this on the board.

- Students only win a point when they splat and say the correct translation.
- The teacher-students continue running Splat at their boards until you decide when to finish.

Variations to the FLA

- Get the teacher-student to copy the English onto the MWB and call out the Target Language, or get them to copy a mix of Target Language and English onto the MWBs.
- Set a short time limit or 'first to five points winner' with the winning student in each pair at the MWB moving to another board to play against someone else or swapping with the teacher-student so that they are able to have a go too.

Teacher notes

As long as the teacher-students have the means to check the translations you can have every confidence in the teacher-students running the FLA.

A minor practicality: the Target Language words may start to get smudgy from all that splatting on the MWBs. It's not beyond the realms of students' organisational awareness for them to rewrite the word again should this happen …

It is not essential that the language copied onto the MWBs should be identical to that on the main board. As long as the students are practising familiar vocabulary, and as long as the teacher-students have a copy of the English for the words being splatted, then a group could use any list of relevant vocabulary.

24 Front-to-Front (FLA)

This FLA is a variation of Paul Ginnis's Back-to-Back, in which two students sit with their backs to each other. One student describes a visual image to their listening partner, who tries to make an exact copy based on what they hear their partner saying. Ginnis suggests its use for languages thus:

> *The exercise could be conducted in a* modern foreign language. *For example, the cross-section of a house showing the position of different rooms, or routes on a town plan, or the items on different shelves of a refrigerator, or furniture in a room, or descriptions of people.*[23]

The Back-to-Back tool is about transmitting information from one student with privileged information to another naïve student, usually describing visual images. Front-to-Front employs a similar principle: the students face each other with one student able to see the board at the front, whilst the other student cannot see it as they have their back to it.

I use Back-to-Back with visual images, and Front-to-Front with reading, speaking and writing text in the Target Language. Some lesson-long FLAs involving reading, speaking and writing text can benefit from the Front-to-Front technique. For example, the Dictation Dictation Retranslation (FLA #36) has students working Front-to-Front.

---

[23] Ginnis, (2002) p. 69.

Why Front-to-Front for text? Because when one student is writing in the Target Language I sometimes want the other student to be able to see what is being written. Also, if students are facing one another both will be able to hear the other more clearly.

Find two short Target Language texts and type them on separate PowerPoint slides. The students work in pairs: A is looking at the board and B has their back to it. Student A speaks (dictates) the Target Language paragraph to B, who writes down the Target Language. B may ask A up to five questions, such as, 'How is x spelled?', 'Can you speak more slowly please?' or 'Please can you repeat?' These questions must be in the Target Language.

After ten minutes of dictating and copying, the students reverse roles and the process is repeated with the second Target Language text projected onto the board. Finally, the students swap books, you show both Target Language texts on the board, and the students mark each other's texts for accuracy, awarding a mark for every word spelled correctly.

Preparation and resources

- Identify the topic that you want students to practise. Type out two Target Language paragraphs of similar length and perceived level of difficulty, and put them on separate PowerPoint slides. Make a third slide with both paragraphs on it.
- Arrange your classroom seating plan so that students can work as pairs, front-to-front. It may be easier to organise your seating plan into rows and have students in alternate rows with their backs to the board.
- Make sure that those with their backs to the board cannot see the paragraph.

Instructions

- Explain that students are going to sit facing one another. Student A faces the board and reads out the Target Language paragraph to B, who faces them with their back to the board.
- Project the first paragraph. A dictates the paragraph to B, who writes down what they hear in the Target Language.
- A should speak slowly and clearly. B must write the paragraph as accurately as possible. At any point B may ask up to five questions for clarification.
- Model some of the questions that students could ask for clarification. These questions must be in the Target Language.
- After ten minutes the students reverse roles by physically changing places. Then project the second paragraph.

- After another ten minutes ask the students to swap their books over and project both paragraphs onto the board so that they can mark them.
- They should award a mark for every word spelled correctly, total the score and then pass the book back.

Variations to the FLA

- Increase or decrease the number of questions that the student doing the copying can ask.
- Project Target Language sentences instead of paragraphs that the students have to translate into English.
- Project lists of Target Language vocabulary; students must translate each word into English.
- Project sentences with deliberate mistakes that students have to copy down and circle as they are writing.

Teacher notes

Make sure you click the 'no show' button on the projector remote when the students are swapping places so that no student gets a peek at the text that is projected on the board.

25 Better With Letters (FLA)

This FLA is about teamwork, with groups of students working together to spell a word that you call out. It's a frenetic, fast-paced activity which requires students to go back to basics on literacy. It's a great rapport builder, and has an element of competition when it comes to spelling.

Split the class into four groups of students and give each group an alphabet pack. This consists of a set of 30 A6 laminated cards, each of which has a different letter of the alphabet on each side. To accommodate accented letters include all the variations on the same card. So for example, on an A card you will have *a* together with *à á â* and *ä*. On the other side of the card put the letter B. (The C card has both *c* and *ç*, the N card both *n* and *ñ*, the S card both *s* and *ß*, and so on.) Continue to do this for two complete alphabets on 26 cards so that you have two cards with the same letter on. (If your Target Language is Spanish, include a further card with *ch* on one side and *ll* on the other.) Leave the remaining cards blank, so that the students can use them as blanks as they would in Scrabble. Once you have made the packs of letters then it's another resource you will have available at any time in the future.

To run the FLA, project a list of vocabulary onto the board or just give each group dictionaries and textbooks. Call out an English word either from the list on the board or one for which the Target Language meaning has been taught then watch the students frantically trying to find the letters that spell the Target Language word. Once the letters have been found it is just as much fun seeing the students lining themselves in the correct order, holding a letter in each hand to spell the word from left to right as you read it. But it hasn't finished yet: once the students are lined up holding the letters in the correct order they then have to shout out the word they have spelled three times. The first group to do that gets a point. You then call out another word and the process starts all over again.

Preparation and resources

- For each alphabet pack get thirty pieces of A6-size paper or card and print one letter of the alphabet on one side and a different letter on the other, so that you end up with two complete alphabets on 26 cards (27 for Spanish), and four blank cards.
- Put all the accented variations on the same card as the unaccented letter.
- Laminate all the pieces of paper or card.
- Identify a list of Target Language words that you would like to test the students on. This could be a list of key vocabulary as with the VFLAs or a page of vocabulary and phrases in the textbook, a general topic area, or a list that the students have found challenging. Copy the vocabulary or phrases onto a PowerPoint slide and number each item.
- Project the vocabulary or phrases onto the board so that every student can see them.

Instructions

- Divide the class into groups of four and explain that each group has to compete against other groups to spell the Target Language for the English words that you call out.
- Give each group an alphabet pack.
- Say that you are going to call out the English for a word on the board.
- The groups identify the Target Language for the English called out, find the letters to spell the word, and then line up at the front, left to right from your point of view, showing the letters in the correct order.
- They then shout out the word in the Target Language three times.
- The group that does this first scores a point. Repeat with another word.
- A group can also use a maximum of two blanks as substitute letters only if the actual letters have already been used, and they need to tell you what letter (using the Target Language alphabet) they represent.

Variations to the FLA

- Give the groups a time limit to spell the word. If no group has spelled it in the time limit then call out another word.

- Get students writing a sentence spelling a word at a time. They are not allowed to move onto the next word in the sentence until you have checked it. The winning group is the group to have spelled the full sentence.
- Get the students to conduct the FLA in silence. Any group with a student who breaks the silence incurs a very short time penalty.
- Get the students to not only call out the Target Language word when they have spelled it but the Target Language pronunciation for each letter as well, before being able to claim a point.

Teacher notes

You may find that you are short of vowels, so you may want to have multiple copies of those cards.

You may want to have a pack of cards for a particular Target Language, in which case you will not have letters with umlauts, say, on the French pack, or c-cedillas in the German pack, and so on.

26 Fast-Forwarded Learning (FLA)

This FLA gets the students to concentrate on recorded information. It's intended to make students passionately curious about how different types of language knowledge work. In Chapter 1, I mentioned that this FLA doesn't quite fit the strategy of first impart language knowledge, then practise. The *fast-forwarded* part of this FLA is not the physical act of fast-forwarding your clip but rather fast-forwarding to the point at which you want the students to be in a few lessons' time. In so doing you are raising students' expectations.

The idea of recording a clip of yourself (before the lesson) using a tense that the students are not yet familiar with and teaching them how to write two or three sentences with that tense might at first glance seem a little incongruous. The Fast-Forwarded Learning FLA promotes a discussion between students and the teacher about what knowledge students think they would need in order to fill in the gaps to arrive at the point at which you are teaching. Such a discussion gives students an insight into the importance of building on prior knowledge.

Record a clip of yourself teaching a language topic which would normally happen in two or three lessons' time. During the recording provide some cues that will connect to students' prior knowledge. For instance, suppose the students are about to learn the preterite tense in Spanish, of which they have no prior knowledge. In the first lesson of your planned sequence, you want them to know the endings of the preterite tense in the 'I' form for regular -*ar*, -*er* and -*ir* verbs. Record a clip of yourself in an empty classroom teaching how to write two or three sentences in the preterite tense. Start with a time phrase that goes with the first verb you want to put into the preterite tense, then use the correct verb ending (presupposing that students have already been taught how to conjugate verbs in the preterite tense) and then teach the connectives to link what you are teaching to another sentence in the preterite tense. The first part of the explanation at the start of the clip could go something like this:

'Hola, hola, hola. ¿Qué tal? *OK, today we're going to be looking at building two or three sentences using the preterite tense in the "I" form. The first step is to find an appropriate time phrase that matches the tense we're using. So, we could start with one of these time phrases [write on the board two or three different time phrases commonly used with the preterite tense]. Let's choose* ayer, *which means? Yes! ¡Genial! Well done, Tom! It means "yesterday". So, we start with* ayer *[write* Ayer *with a capital on the board]. Next comes the verb in the preterite tense, so let's have a look at some regular verbs. Can anyone tell me any regular infinitives first of all? Brilliant! Well done, Sarah!* Comer *is a regular infinitive; can you remember what it means? Yes, that's right, "to eat". So, we put* comer *after* Ayer *like this [write* comer *on the board]. We can't just leave a time phrase like* Ayer *there followed by an infinitive, so we have to put the verb into the tense to match the time phrase. So, for* comer *we take off the* er *like this [cross the* er *ending off on the board] and then add an* i *with an accent like this [rub out the crossed out* er *and write* í *instead] so now we have* Ayer comí, *which means "Yesterday I ate". The next thing we need to do is to find something that we ate, so, let's choose ... '*

The recording continues with teaching a connective to link *Ayer comí* to another time phrase and finally a different verb and noun. Thus, in your recorded explanation clip you have deliberately missed out teaching how to conjugate different infinitives in the preterite tense and jumped straight into teaching how to build a couple of sentences, assuming students' prior knowledge of the tense formation.

With the class, set the recording up ready to play. Explain that you are going to play a clip of you teaching a lesson that is two or three lessons down the road from where they are at the moment. As they watch the clip, you want them to write down any knowledge that they think they would need for doing what you did on the clip.

Teaching to an empty room lacks interaction, but if you behave as though the students were there, using their names and praising them for the imagined responses that they might make in real life, then Fast-Forwarded Learning is a great way of building up a positive relationship with a class.

Why record a clip? Why not just teach them in real time? This FLA offers a break in the routine, a welcome change. Willingham says that change during lessons is invigorating and gets students to re-focus their attention.[24] Jeff Nevid, in *Teaching the Millennials*, suggests that

---

[24] Willingham, (2009) p. 165.

teachers need to 'grab their students' attention' partly by 'changing what we do during class every ten minutes'.[25] This means continual shifts of focus not only during lessons but across a term and the whole Scheme of Learning.

Another reason for recording a clip is that students can't say 'I don't get it' because they know they can't have that dialogue and interaction with you. In a discussion with the course leader and other trainee teachers on the languages PGCE, we talked about how strange it was that students might talk or display off-task behaviours during speaking, reading or writing activities but when it came to doing a listening activity students generally remained quiet and focused. The students know they have to concentrate as there are no second chances. The same principle applies to the Scheme of Learning Trailer (FLA #27).

Preparation and resources

- Identify a tense in the Target Language that you want the students to know and understand which you would normally introduce two or three lessons further on. For example, you presuppose that they already know how to form the tense, and are now showing how this applies to building sentences using connectives.
- In an empty classroom, set up a camera and record yourself teaching a five- or ten-minute clip describing how you would use this tense with time phrases and connectives to build some sentences (as in the example above). Make the recording using your phone, a Flip camera or one of the many alternative options for recording video.
- Set the clip up ready to play on the projector at the front of the class.

Instructions

- Explain to the class that you are going to play a video clip of you teaching part of a lesson that comes from the future, describing how to use a tense with time phrases and connectives in creating sentences. Say that you would normally teach this in two or three lessons' time, and the clip assumes the students already know the tense you are using.
- During the clip you want the students to write down at least five things that they would need to know in order to be able to write the sentences demonstrated in the clip.
- Model some of the things they could write down, for example, 'I need to know why an ending has been added' or 'I need to know other time phrases to use' and so on.

---

[25] Jeff Nevid, (2011) 'Teaching the Millennials', (*Association for Psychological Science*) Observer Vol. 24, No. 5 May/June.

- Play the clip. Then get the students to feed back to you what knowledge they think they would need for writing the sentences you modelled in the clip.
- Depending on how the discussion goes, now teach the actual tense conjugations!

Variations to the FLA

- Adapt the FLA to other areas of the language: record and play a clip about adjectives when students are familiar only with the Target Language nouns.

Teacher notes

You might think that a YouTube clip would work just as well for this FLA. However, in recording your own clip you obviously have far more control, which means you can tailor the teaching to the exact point at which you want the students to be in a few lessons' time.

The first time I ran this FLA everything went well apart from the fact that I hadn't modelled what I wanted the students to write precisely enough. Just saying 'note down what it is that you think you need to do' was too vague. Thereafter I used more precise modelling and got the students to give me more concrete responses about what they thought they needed.

Leave plenty of time for the discussion afterwards. Talk to the students about the endings for the tense. Discuss how to do this. Cover the *knowing what* and the *knowing how* of declarative and procedural knowledge respectively, and explain to the students that each type of knowledge involves a different type of performance.[26]

What really matters is that you have high expectations of what the students can do, and you have faith in their being able to write these sentences. Showing students where the learning road map is leading might also help to incentivise the students to grapple engagingly with the initial teaching of the actual tense conjugation.

---

[26] Ambrose et al., (2010) p. 18.

27 Scheme of Learning Trailer (FLA)

The Scheme of Learning Trailer FLA is based on the same principle as the Fast-Forwarded Learning (FLA #26). Do all the things that you do for Fast-Forwarded Learning except this time record a five- to ten-minute clip summarising some of the language and grammatical features that appear on the Scheme of Learning for the next half-term.

Look at the Scheme of Learning in terms of the content, and record a clip where you teach parts of what is to come. For example:

> *'OK, the first few lessons of this module are all about free time. So we'll be learning and practising sports- and hobbies-related vocabulary here. We'll be looking at two different verbs in the present tense and learning how to talk about the sports you play and the hobbies that you do, as well as learning why this is important. We'll be looking at frequency phrases to say how often we play the sports and do the hobbies. For instance, we'll look at adverbs such as* normalement *[write* normalement *on the board] and* tous les jours *[write* tous les jours *on the board] to do this. After this we'll be looking at making arrangements and … '*

Continue your commentary including two, three or even four more different topics.

This FLA provides an opportunity for the students to ask about and discuss the language presented in the clip. When you play the clip to the students explain that it details what is on the Scheme of Learning for the next few weeks, and that you want them to note down at least five questions to do with what they will be learning (to promote curiosity) in order to solve 'the problem'. This problem is what you want the students to focus on; for example, how to write two or three sentences using some of the language referred to in the clip. The idea comes from *Creating Outstanding Classrooms* in which Knight and Benson discuss the 'Fertile Question', which they define as:

> *A planning device for knitting together a sequence of lessons, so that all of the learning activities – teacher exposition, narrative, source-work, role-play, plenary – all move towards the resolution of an interesting and meaningful historical/scientific/mathematical/RE problem.*[27]

Both this FLA and the Fast-Forwarded Learning FLA share some of the characteristics of the Fertile Question approach. The problem to be resolved could be how to write a paragraph about what you do in your free time, or how to describe a distant relative to a fellow student, and so on.

Model some of the questions that the students could note down, such as, 'Why is there different language to talk about sports that you play and hobbies that you do?' or 'What other ways are there to describe how often you play a sport?'

The FLA is also designed to get students thinking about the meaning of the language coming up in the next few weeks. It can help (just as with a film trailer) to get students excited about what the Scheme of Learning has to offer. Its aim is to promote a wider discussion about the topic and the relevant language content.

Preparation and resources

- Identify the section of the Scheme of Learning that you want to prepare a trailer for, such as the next half-term.
- Set up a camera at the back of an empty classroom and record yourself teaching a five- or ten-minute clip describing what is coming up on the Scheme of Learning, using examples as described above.
- Set the clip up ready to play on the projector at the front of the class.

---

[27] O. Knight and D. Benson, (2014) *Creating Outstanding Classrooms: A Whole-School Approach*, Abingdon, Routledge. p. 74.

Instructions

- Tell the class that you are going to play a video clip of you describing the upcoming part of the Scheme of Learning in which you talk about what will be coming up in the next few weeks.
- Specify the problem in terms of a 'how-to' (as above).
- During the clip they should write down at least five things: either what they would need to know in order to use the language and the topics you discuss for solving the problem, or five questions they would need answers for.
- Model some of the things that students could write down (as above).
- Play the clip. Get the students to feed back to you on what knowledge they think they would need.
- Discuss what you and the class could do about solving the problem.

Variations to the FLA

- Vary the section of the Scheme of Learning that you use for the clip.
- Record a longer clip and give students a blank Scheme of Learning to fill in.

Teacher notes

This is a good way of priming the students for what is to come in the near future. For example, suppose that in week four of the Scheme of Learning they find out how to describe themselves in the Target Language. If during the class discussion a student asks if that means that they'll be learning about celebrities, tell them that it does. That could then spark off another student asking you how they would say what colour their favourite celebrity's eyes are in French. You answer such questions there and then, so that when the actual lesson on describing themselves and others comes round, some weeks later, you can connect the learning in that lesson to the discussion about the celebrity's eye colour in the earlier lesson. Although such spontaneous student behaviour cannot be planned, it is still a potential feature to look out for during the FLA.

Getting the students to write five questions during the playing of the clip relates to the second of the eight stages of the Fertile Question approach, which is partly characterised by letting students choose questions that they would like to pose in order to answer the Fertile Question.[28]

---

[28] Knight and Benson, (2014) p. 77.

28 Seeing Double (FLA)

This is the third FLA in the spirit of the Fast-Forwarded Learning and the Scheme of Learning Trailer FLAs. This time you record yourself teaching a grammar point: a tense, adjective formation, adverbs, or whatever, and then play this clip to the students. This is a great way to grab students' attention and get them focused, as well as being a great rapport builder. When I first tried this with a class the students told me that they preferred the recorded me to the live me!

Suppose you record a clip on how to form the future tense. You play the clip twice: the first time the students just watch and listen; the second time they make notes. However, simply saying 'make notes on how to form the tense' is too vague, so be more precise. Say that you want them to note down the endings of the tense, how the endings are conjugated, when the tense is used and which are the most common irregular verbs that do not follow the pattern.

Why record yourself teaching it and playing it?

For the same reasons as with Fast-Forwarded Learning (FLA #26): you are providing novelty, and you are utilising the principle of having a listening activity in which the students focus more on the task because they know that what they are hearing is ephemeral and they cannot interact with it. If they don't focus on what is being said in the clip they lose out. It seems odd to be championing a lack of interaction, but it is the enforced lack of interaction and the teacher's judicious use of when to employ this FLA which help make it effective. Of course, as with any activity, if you overuse it, it becomes counterproductive.

Preparation and resources

- Identify a tense in the Target Language that you want the students to learn.
- Set up a camera at the back of an empty classroom and record yourself teaching a five- or ten-minute clip explaining the tense.
- Set the clip up ready to play on the projector at the front of the class.

Instructions

- Explain to the class that you are going to play a video clip of you teaching a tense. You will play it twice, but you won't pause it.
- The first time through you want the students to just watch it. The second time you want them to write down the *what, how, when* and *which* of the tense as described above.
- Model some of the things that students could write down. For example, 'It's used when you want to say things like "I will go" in the Target Language.'
- Play the clip twice. Then get the students to feed their responses back to you. If students need the clip playing again then do so one more time. Have a discussion about how the tense works and how the FLA went.
- Depending on how the discussion goes, teach the tense again 'live' so that students have the opportunity to see double – and then compare which version of you they prefer.

Variations to the FLA

- Get an older student (with a secure enough knowledge of the tense) to be recorded on the clip teaching the tense.
- Record a clip of two or three tenses and discuss the features of each tense afterwards.

Teacher notes

Play the clip as the students are coming in to class as a way of setting the scene at the start of the lesson and as a way of promoting curiosity amongst the students about what is going to happen.

29 Pic 'n' Mix (FLA)

With the Pic 'n' Mix FLA the students work in groups and attempt to assemble some randomly selected Target Language words and phrases to make a grammatically correct sentence. Students have to think about the meaning of the words they have picked out and work out if and how they can be combined.

This FLA requires some initial resource-making, but once they are made they're another resource in the language locker.

Put four boxes at the front of the class. Each box contains dozens of different Target Language words or phrases, each on a small piece of card.

- Box one: a variety of time / frequency phrases. For Spanish, these could be *el año pasado, ayer, normalmente,* and so on.
- Box two: different subjects; for example, in Spanish these could be *mi familia, nosotros/ nosotras, mi amigo/a,* and so on.
- Box three: a selection of regular infinitives, such as *comer, beber, hablar.*
- Box four: adds extra detail with a mix of nouns – *una limonada, una hamburguesa* – and longer phrases – *cuando tengo el tiempo, con mis amigos/con mis amigas, con mi familia, en un restaurante* and so on.

Each group of three assigns the customary roles: runner, scribe and textbook and dictionary researcher. The runner visits the boxes at the front of the class, the scribe does the writing, and the textbook and dictionary researcher checks on meaning.

The runner visits all four boxes in turn and picks out a time phrase, a subject, an infinitive and an extra detail card without looking at them. The group then work together to write a logical and grammatically correct sentence on their mini-whiteboard or MWB based on the four cards they have selected. Once completed, they call you over to check that what they have written makes sense.

If it's nonsense, tell the group which cards they should take back to a box to replace. For every sentence that does make sense the group scores a point. The runner goes back to the boxes, takes four different cards and returns the used cards to the correct box. The winning group is the first to get to five points by producing five different sentences.

Because you've made boxes of infinitives and time phrases the groups will have to do some thinking: they have to conjugate the infinitive that they have picked from the box to match the time phrase that they picked out. Suppose that a runner picks out *normalmente, mi amigo, comer* and *en un restaurante*. To write a well-formed sentence with these words, they first need to work out which tense to use with *normalmente* and conjugate the infinitive *comer* to match the subject *mi amigo*.

Preparation and resources

- Print a variety of different time/frequency phrases, subjects, regular infinitives and extra details onto A4 cards and then cut them up. You can duplicate phrases.
- Get four smallish plastic boxes and label each one (with a permanent marker) according to the cards that you put in them: 'time/frequency phrases', 'subjects', 'regular infinitives' and 'extra details'.
- Put the boxes of cards at the front of the class.
- Arrange your seating plan so that groups of three can work together on a MWB at a base on a set of desks.

Instructions

- Explain to the students that they will be working in groups of three with the customary roles as described above.
- Each group finds a base by one of the MWBs. The scribe has a marker pen.
- The runner in each group takes one card from each of the four boxes at the front and returns to their group.
- The group then work out how to write a sentence on the MWB based on the cards they have. If the four cards would clearly not make a well-formed sentence then the runner returns the cards and picks out some different ones.

- They must conjugate the infinitive according to the subject and the time/frequency phrase cards. The sentence that a group constructs must make logical and grammatical sense. Model examples of sentences that do and do not make sense.
- When a group thinks that they have written a well-formed sentence, they call you over to check it. If it's correct they leave their sentence on the MWB and win a point. Their runner goes back to the boxes, picks out another card from each box, and returns the original cards to the correct boxes.
- The group repeats the process for their next sentence.
- If a group calls you over to check a sentence that isn't correct then you feed back to that group on how to fix it.
- The first group to get five points (five correct sentences) wins.

Variations to the FLA

- Get the students to write their sentences on mini-whiteboards to show you.
- Simplify the FLA to practise one tense and have two boxes: subjects and infinitives.
- Get groups to make crazy sentences instead. Award two points for particularly crazy sentences.
- Nominate four students in class as quality-controllers: they stand in front of the boxes and ensure that the runner puts the cards back in the right boxes.
- Have groups of four students. Each student in the group has to go to a specific box to get the card and bring it back to their group's base.
- Add an extension task. After a group writes a correct sentence, say they can only have a point and move onto the next by adding their own opinion phrase to their sentence.
- Once a class has completed five sentences tell them that to win they now have to use a connective to link all of their sentences together to make a logically and grammatically correct paragraph.

Teacher notes

Hmm ... how to ensure that the students put the cards back in the right boxes:

- Label each box clearly!
- Put each box in a different corner of the room.
- Use the quality-controller option above.
- Use four different coloured boxes.
- Depending on time and budget constraints, colour-code the cards so that each box has cards of the same colour, making it easy to see if any card has found its way into the wrong box.

30 Task Corner (FLA)

Welcome to Task Corner, the place where spaced practice is celebrated!

In a study involving surgeons, two groups of surgeons had four lessons in microsurgery, each lesson included some teaching and then some practice. One group took all four lessons in a single day; the other group had the four lessons spaced out with a week between them. When tested, the surgeons who had their lessons spaced out did better in all areas of performance than those who had had all of their lessons in one day. The reason, according to Brown et al., is that consolidation is needed in order to get new learning to stick in our long-term memory. In that way, 'memory traces' are bolstered and attached to prior knowledge, and this can take several days.[29]

With this in mind, this FLA focuses on spaced retrieval practice and is used with a class over a few lessons. The FLA is intended to create a discussion with the students over the benefits of spaced practice.

The process is this: towards the mid-point of a sequence of two or three lessons where the students have been learning some topic-related vocabulary, give each student a sticky note (or a Magic Sticky Note™ so that the notes can be reused), project a list of vocabulary that the students have been learning onto the board (as with the VFLAs), and get the students in pairs

---

[29] Brown et al., (2014) p. 49.

as A and B. The students ask each other which words they now know the English meaning of that they didn't know a few lessons ago. Encourage students to discuss their favourite and least favourite words.

Ask A to write any six Target Language words onto the sticky note that B didn't know at the start but does now. B does the same for A. The students then write their partner's name at the bottom of the note, and this note now becomes the task for the corner. All the students stick these notes in the designated Task Corner and sit down again.

Why have the students written their partner's vocabulary task and not their own? Because the discussion surrounding what has been learned should be shared between students, and because by discussing their favourite and least favourite words the students are thinking about meaning. There is also a slightly less subjective feel about writing the vocabulary for someone else's test!

In two lessons' time (allowing time for spaced retrieval practice) you want them to come into class, take the sticky note with their name on and write the English next to the six Target Language words on the note. If you stick enough MWBs on the walls then students can write the Target Language and English on these and sign their names underneath. The students with full marks win a prize. Afterwards, you discuss with the students the merits of spaced practice and spaced practice retrieval.

Given that this is vocabulary-based you might wonder how it has made it into the FLAs. It's because the variations for this FLA could include many other tasks. For instance, the students could discuss how to write sentences in a particular tense, and then write a task on a sticky note for another student based on that student's procedural knowledge of how to use that tense. For example, 'Write down three examples of the present tense, together with an opinion.' In two to three lessons' time the student goes to the Task Corner, retrieves their sticky note and proves that they can indeed write down three examples of the present tense, together with an opinion. They write their examples on the MWB or on the back of the same sticky note, and show you.

Preparation and resources

- Get a pack of sticky notes or Magic Sticky Notes™ (if using MWBs, stick two or three boards up in a corner of the class).
- Identify the group of Target Language words or phrases that you want the students to use as their task for the Task Corner. This could be a list of vocabulary such as those used for the VFLAs, a page of vocabulary and phrases in the textbook, a general topic

area, or a list that the students have found challenging. Copy the vocabulary or phrases onto a PowerPoint slide and number each item.
- Project the vocabulary or phrases onto the board so that every student can see them.

Instructions

- Students work in pairs as A and B. Hand each student a sticky note and ask them to discuss which words they have learned the meaning of in this lesson. Ask them to discuss their favourite and least favourite words. Student A writes on a sticky note the Target Language for six words that B has learned this lesson; A puts B's name underneath. B does the same for A.
- Stick the sticky notes up in the Task Corner.
- Explain that in two lessons' time the students will answer their task. They come into class, take the sticky note with their name on and write the Target Language and the English meaning.
- When that has happened, project the vocabulary with the English so the students can mark their task. Ask them to feed back to you how many words they got right.
- Discuss how this FLA went with the students.

Variations to the FLA

- Vary the tasks that students write on a sticky note. Instead of Target Language vocabulary get them to write down the endings of a tense that has just been learned, an English translation for a Target Language sentence, or a mixture of vocabulary and tense endings.
- Split the class into two with equal numbers of students on both sides and run the FLA as described above. Add up the total number of vocabulary that the students get right per side. The side of the class with the most vocabulary gains wins.

Teacher notes

If you get the students to set tasks which are not vocabulary-based, then model a selection of tasks they could use which relate to the learning in previous lessons.

31 Before, Now, After and Forever (FLA)

This FLA provides practice in using different verb tenses. The students describe images using past, present and future tenses. This is another activity designed to build students' confidence in speaking.

The students describe the Before image using the past tense, the Now in the present tense, and the After with the future tense. Oh, and the Forever is the enduring effect that the activity will hopefully have on the students' progress and engagement.

Find three images to do with a topic the students have been learning about and put all three onto a PowerPoint slide. Arrange them left to right with the Before image on the left. Add some support language around the images to help students to speak about them. This FLA works in a similar way to Speak-Off (FLA #1) except students work in pairs as A and B, each speaking for thirty seconds using each tense in turn to describe the images.

Suppose the students have been learning about the topic of Home Town and Region. You arrange images of a village (Before), a town (Now) and a city (After) on a PowerPoint slide. You then add some relevant Target Language phrases around the images, the English for which would be 'In the past there was … ' and 'We used to have … ' for the Before image, 'Now there is … ' and 'We have … ' for the Now image, and 'In the future there will be … ' and 'We will have … ' for the Future image. Students have access to the Target Language on the slide and a textbook opened at a double-page spread of vocabulary and phrases to do with the Home Town and Region topic as extra support.

Student A talks about each image for thirty seconds; B does the timing. If A is successful, they win a point. If A struggles describing an image or slips into a different tense, they are not awarded a point. It is at B's discretion whether or not A has spoken well enough.

Preparation and resources

- Identify the topic that you want students to practise language on, such as Home Town and Region. Find three relevant images which could relate to the past, present and future, and copy these onto a PowerPoint slide. Leave space on the slide to add relevant Target Language phrases for each image.
- Arrange your classroom seating plan so that students can work in pairs.
- Project the three images and Target Language onto the board so that every student can see them.
- Get a set of textbooks with a double page of vocabulary related to the topic you are practising.

Instructions

- Tell the students that they will work in pairs as A and B. Each student talks about each picture using a different tense for thirty seconds.
- Student A starts by talking about the image on the left using the past tense. If they keep going for thirty seconds they win a point. B records the score.
- B's job is to listen. If they decide that A has kept going in the correct tense for thirty seconds, they award a point. If A hasn't kept speaking for thirty seconds, has not used the correct tense, or has used the same chunk phrase more than three times they will not be awarded a point.
- After thirty seconds B signals to A to describe the next picture, and so on.
- The roles are then reversed. Finally they add up the scores, and the winning student is the one with the most points.

Variations to the FLA

- Once both students have had a go at going from the past to the future, have them do it again but go from the future to the past (from right to left).
- Vary the pictures (and topics) you use. Have a set of holiday destination pictures, or three different educational establishments (primary school for the past image, secondary

for the present image and for the future use three smaller images to represent the world of work).

- Vary the number of phrases on the slide; following spaced practice of the topic with this FLA, have fewer chunk phrases each time you practise it again with that class.
- Instead of a PowerPoint slide, use Flickr to show some pictures and provide the students with a handout of vocabulary to support them to describe each one.

Teacher notes

Before, Now, After and Forever uses a similar principle to Speak-Off (FLA #1) except that there is more of a focus on practising tenses.

32 Treasured Language Hunt (FLA)

This FLA is based on an old favourite which has been tweaked and adapted to join the band of FLAs. Essentially, clues in the Target Language are hidden around the classroom, and groups compete against other groups to find these clues and then complete the tasks referred to.

The groups assign the usual roles of scribe, runner and textbook/dictionary researcher. The Treasured Language Hunt FLA can take up a large proportion of the lesson, if not all of it.

The numbered clues are written on small cards. Tasks are also numbered and placed in envelopes which are then hidden around the room. Each clue and task should have the instructions written in the Target Language. Have the same number of clues and tasks as the number of groups. Make multiple copies of the clues and tasks so that several groups can work on them at the same time.

Hide the envelopes containing the tasks around the classroom. The teacher starts off with all the clue cards and gives one clue at a time (in any order) to each runner, who takes it back to their group to work out. Each clue should hint at where the task has been hidden. Once a group has solved the clue they send their runner to find the matching task envelope. The runner removes a task card, replaces the envelope and returns to their group, where they complete the task together.

When a group finishes the task the runner gets it checked by you. If it's correct, tick off this task. If not, give feedback to the runner on how to fix what they've done and then send them back to their group to do so. The first group to complete all the tasks wins the Treasured Language Hunt FLA.

What to put on a task and clue

The clues hint at where the task envelopes have been put. Some Spanish examples:

1. *Pista 1: La primera pista, estoy pegado al ordenador.*
2. *Pista 2: Busca en uno de los rincones de la sala PG1.*

Tasks can be based on any topic, and should be short and sharp: two or three words or sentences to translate, or a reading exercise from the textbook. For example:

1. *Tarea 1: Escribe el inglés para estas palabras.*
   Los vuelos =
   El vidrio =
2. *Tarea 2: Ejercicio 3 en la página 31 del libro.*

The instructions below assume seven groups of three students but this can be adapted.

Preparation and resources

- Decide on the tasks first: an exercise from a textbook, a short translation, etc. Write the tasks in the Target Language on separate pieces of card, numbering each one.
- Make the same number of copies of each task as the number of groups. Put each set into a separate envelope and label it with the task number.
- Choose hiding places for the envelopes around the classroom and devise some appropriate clues. Write a matching numbered clue for each task in the Target Language and make the same number of copies as there are groups.
- Arrange each set of clues in separate numbered piles on your desk.
- Hide the task envelopes around the classroom.
- Make sure there is easy access for runners to move around the room.
- Create a scoring chart with the number of each task down one side and the number of groups across the top.

Instructions

- The students get into groups of three, assign the roles of scribe, runner and textbook/ dictionary researcher, and find a base.
- Explain to the class there are seven tasks to complete and the first group to complete all seven is the winner. The tasks are written in the Target Language.

- Hidden around the classroom are seven envelopes, each containing one of these tasks. There are seven copies of each task, one for each group.
- The groups send their runner to you to collect a clue to take back to their group. The clue is written in the Target Language and indicates where the corresponding task envelope is.
- Once a group has figured out where the envelope is, their runner retrieves a copy of the task and returns to their group. When the group has completed the task, the runner brings it to you to check.
- If the task is correct tick the task off for that group. If not, give feedback to the runner on what their group needs to do to fix it.
- Groups can only work on one task at a time, and it must be checked by you before moving on to another. The tasks can be completed in any order.

Variations to the FLA

- Vary the number of clues and tasks.
- Vary how you communicate the clues to the students. Instead of having the clues written down on cards, explain that you are going to speak the clue in the Target Language to the runner who then has to relay this back to their group. If they forget, they have to come back and ask you to repeat it using Target Language requests.
- Introduce a time limit to complete each task, and put the time allowed at the top of each card. If a group don't complete the task in time then they have to change tasks.
- Make it a school-wide Treasured Language Hunt (Health and Safety permitting, of course) with tasks hidden around school.
- Instead of tasks in envelopes you could use QR codes (Quick Response codes, like bar codes) where you type the task onto a QR code and hide these around the room (or the school). Provided that the students have an iPad (or are allowed to use their phones) with a downloaded app for reading QR codes, such as Kaywa Reader, then that will guide them to their task.

Teacher notes

Because students see other students finding tasks around the class they might think that they can skip getting a clue and go straight to the task. This is not allowed; they have to first take a clue and demonstrate that they have worked out where the task is before they can go and get it.

33 Front–To–Front Who Is It (FLA)

This FLA is a variation on Front-to-Front (FLA #24), but it couldn't be included in the Variations section as it needs a greater depth of explanation. Students need to listen carefully to answers to questions in order to identify the name of the subject.

Project a list of Target Language questions to do with a topic, such as Personal Details, shown here:

1. *¿Qué tal?*	5. *¿Tienes hermanos?*
2. *¿Cuándo es tu cumpleaños?*	6. *¿Dónde vives?*
3. *¿Cuántos años tienes?*	7. *¿Cómo te llamas?*
4. *¿Tienes animales en casa?*	

The last question is always 'What is your name?' The students work in pairs as A and B, front-to-front, with A facing the board and B with their back to it. Both students copy the list of questions (with the questions remaining the same throughout the FLA).

Create a document with about thirty different boxes, each filled with possible Target Language answers to the questions above. Number each box. B has a copy of this document.

The responses in each box are not identical; at least one piece of information is different in each box. However, the answer to question 7 (the name) is never given, as that is the information which has to be discovered.

1	**2**
1. *Bien.*	1. *Bien.*
2. *Mi cumpleaños es el veinte de agosto.*	2. *Mi cumpleaños es el veinte de agosto.*
3. *Tengo quince años.*	3. *Tengo quince años.*
4. *Tengo un gato.*	4. *Tengo un gato.*
5. *Sí, tengo dos hermanos.*	5. *Sí, tengo una hermana.*
6. *Vivo en Londres.*	6. *Vivo en Madrid.*
7. *Me llamo …*	7. *Me llamo …*
3	**4**
1. *Bien.*	1. *Bien.*
2. *Mi cumpleaños es el veinte de agosto.*	2. *Mi cumpleaños es el veinte de agosto.*
3. *Tengo catorce años.*	3. *Tengo catorce años.*
4. *Tengo dos gatos.*	4. *Tengo un gato.*
5. *Sí, tengo dos hermanos.*	5. *Sí, tengo dos hermanos.*
6. *Vivo en Barcelona.*	6. *Vivo en Valencia.*
7. *Me llamo …*	7. *Me llamo …*

Choose any twelve of the thirty boxes on the document and put each one of them on a separate PowerPoint slide. However, instead of leaving the name blank you fill in an imaginary name for these twelve slides. Project the first slide onto the board.

Student B asks the questions from page 203 in the order they appear. A looks at the board and gives those answers shown on the board to the questions B asks.

Set a time limit of one minute for B to find the correct box on their document according to the information given by A. When B has found the description that matches what A is saying, B writes that name on the document. If necessary, B can repeat questions if they are within the time limit. After six slides the students swap roles.

Preparation and resources

- Identify the topic that you want students to practise, such as Personal Details.
- Type out some Target Language questions to do with the topic onto a PowerPoint slide, making sure 'What is your name?' is the last question.
- Create a document with about thirty boxes, each giving a slight variation in the answers (differing one or two pieces of information). Number each box.
- Make a half-class set of this document.
- Choose any twelve of the boxes from the document and copy the content of each box onto a separate PowerPoint slide.
- On each slide add a different name as the last response. This will be the last piece of information to be read out.
- Arrange your classroom seating plan so that it allows students to work as pairs with one student with their back to the board and their partner facing them. It may be better to organise your seating plan into rows and divide the class into halves so that students in one row turn their backs to the board and work with students in the next row, who remain facing the board.
- Project the first slide of the PowerPoint onto the board so that the A students can see the responses.

Instructions

- The students copy down the questions in the same order they appear on the board (or provide them with a handout). They sit facing one another with A facing the board and B with their back to it.
- Give each student B a copy of the document with the boxes of thirty different answers.
- B asks A the list of questions in order. Their task is to find out who is being described on the PowerPoint slide.
- A answers the questions according to what they read on the board.
- When B thinks they have found the matching box on their document they write in the person's name after *Me llamo …*
- B can ask the questions as many times as they like but each slide will only be shown for one minute. After that, show the next slide, and the process repeats.
- After six slides the students swap roles.

Variations to the FLA

- Vary the time limit on finding the person being described.
- Vary the number of boxes and descriptions you use on a document. Vary the amount of language you change in each box.
- Vary the topic: use topics such as Holidays with questions such as, 'Where do you go on holiday?', 'Whom do you go with?' and so on, still making sure that the last question is 'What is your name?'
- Conduct the FLA in groups of four with two students taking turns to ask a question and two students taking turns to answer a question.
- Make it competitive: the pair that have found the most 'people' at the end of the FLA win.

Teacher notes

Devise questions that would elicit answers from any language content on any syllabus. As long as 'What is your name?' is used you could adapt this to any topic.

So that students are not sitting passively once they have found who is being described before the time limit is up, tell them to keep speaking and rehearsing the dialogue as extra practice. Another extension task is to translate the description.

If B has identified the name based on the first few questions, they might be tempted to write the name down. Explain that they can only put down the name after all the information has been exchanged.

34 Pronuncistation Funology (FLA)

The Pronuncistation Funology FLA is based on two things: how well students can spell a Target Language word from listening to a recording, and how well they can understand the pronunciation of the word based on how it is transcribed in the dictionary.

This FLA requires students to have some prior knowledge of sound-spelling links in the Target Language; because students look up words in dictionaries, they need to understand the International Phonetic Association symbols used. The importance of phonetic transcription is highlighted by John Wells.[30]

In the past, Target Language pronunciation had become something of an afterthought that I would bung onto the end of a lesson: 'Oh, and remember to pronounce your *v* as a *b*, OK?' Since then, I have become rather more fastidious, and, to use the students' parlance as regards the importance of pronunciation these days, it is most definitely a case of 'I get it now.'

With this FLA, choose some Target Language words that the students have not yet come across. These can be from a topic such as School Uniform, or from any topic covered in the Scheme of Learning.

Create a handout of just the English for these words, and another of the dictionary's phonetic transcription of the Target Language together with the English meaning. For example: /ʒyp/ –

---

[30] John Wells, (1996) 'Why Phonetic Transcription is Important', *Journal of the Phonetic Society of Korea*, No. 31–32:239–242, December. See http://www.phon.ucl.ac.uk/home/wells/whytranscription.htm.

skirt or /pãtalɔ̃/ – trousers. Make two copies of these phonetic transcription handouts and fold them so that the top of the sheet acts as a flap which hides what is written. Stick these on the wall in two corners of the room. These are the two Transcription Pronuncistations. Make sure that when you stick the folded sheets up the students cannot see what is on them without lifting the flap.

Record a sound file using a Dictaphone or phone, carefully pronouncing each Target Language word three times and then saying what the word means. Copy the sound file onto another Dictaphone (or a laptop if you only have one Dictaphone) and put the Dictaphones on tables in the other two corners of the classroom. These are the two Dictaphone Pronuncistations.

The students, in groups of three, find a base in the classroom and assign the following roles: pronuncistation director/scribe (who remains at the group's base, does the writing and tells the other two students in their group which corner to go to next), word collector one and word collector two. One word collector goes to the corner to read the dictionary transcription for the words and their English meanings; the other goes to listen to the pronunciation of the words and their English meanings. The pronuncistation director/scribe in each group has a copy of the handout with just the English on. They tell the word collectors which English words they don't have a Target Language spelling for yet.

The aim for each group is to accurately spell the Target Language for as many of the English words on the pronuncistation director/scribe's document as they can.

Set a twenty-minute time limit for this. Then show the list of English and the correct spelling of the Target Language for each word. The groups mark their lists and tell you their scores. The group with the most Target Language words spelled correctly wins.

Finally, discuss with the students which words they found most difficult to spell in the Target Language. Find out if it was more or less difficult listening to the pronunciation than reading the dictionary's transcription of the words.

This is a good FLA to get students discussing meaning and helps raise awareness of the importance of pronunciation!

Preparation and resources

- Identify a set of Target Language words that the students have not yet learned. Type out just the English for these on one document. Make enough copies for each group of three.
- Make another copy with the English and the dictionary phonetic transcription of each Target Language word. Make two copies, fold them in half and stick one in each corner of the classroom.

- Record yourself pronouncing each Target Language word three times and then saying the English. Copy the recording so it's on two Dictaphones (or a laptop).
  - Put the Dictaphones on tables in the other two corners of the classroom.

Instructions

- The students get into groups of three, find a base and assign the following roles: pronuncistation director/scribe, word collector one and word collector two. Describe the roles as above.
- Give each group a handout with a list of English words. The task for each group is to find the Target Language for these words.
- Explain that you have put Dictaphones in two corners of the classroom. On each there is a recording of you pronouncing the Target Language for the English words on the handout.
- In the other two corners of the classroom there are pieces of folded-over paper with the list of the English words and the dictionary's phonetic transcriptions for each word. The transcriptions use the International Phonetic Alphabet.
- The groups have twenty minutes to get as many Target Language spellings for the words as possible. The pronuncistation director/scribe sends their word collectors to get the words from both corners. However, they are not allowed to take notepads with them; they have to remember how the word is transcribed or pronounced.
- Once a word collector has memorised the pronunciation or transcription they return to base and give this information to the pronuncistation director/scribe, who then writes down how they think the word is spelled.
- At the end of twenty minutes show the list of English with the correct spelling of the words and the groups mark their words accordingly. The group with the most correct Target Language spellings wins Pronuncistation Funology.

Variations to the FLA

- Get involved yourself by acting as a pronuncistation. The students come and ask you how to pronounce the Target Language word that their pronuncistation director has asked them to get.

Teacher notes

It is challenging for many native English speakers to acquire the authentic pronunciation and tonality of a native speaker of a Target Language. Therefore, when making the recording, get a native speaker to record the words instead of you (alternatively, use recordings from an online audio dictionary).

If queues form at the Dictaphone pronuncistations, impose a time limit. Depending on your budget you could get another Dictaphone and a pair of headphones for each one so that more students could be listening to a recording at any one time.

35 Five-Tense Blaster (FLA)

The aim of the Five-Tense Blaster FLA is to move students from practising procedural knowledge of how to form five different tenses to demonstrating their ability to use the 'I' form of each tense in writing a logical and grammatically correct paragraph. (Only use this after students have been taught the endings for the five tenses.) This is a lesson-long FLA with a number of processes which involve the students working individually, then in groups, then as pairs within the group, then back as a group again. It's possible to tweak or shorten this FLA if you want to incorporate it as part of other activities in your lesson.

The idea for this FLA was inspired by the following two views:

> *Learning is often just hard bloody work. Drilling is an essential part of memorisation in some aspects of education.*[31]

> *So how is automaticity achieved? Mainly through extended practice and exposure to the Target Language. There are certainly messages for the foreign language teacher. One is that some of the form-based practice drills which we associate with discredited 'behaviourist approaches' to language learning may not have been entirely useless after all.*[32]

---

[31] Bennett, (2013) p. 127.

[32] Field in Driscoll et al., (2013) p. 24.

The Five-Tense Blaster FLA is about acquiring automaticity. It gives students the confidence to apply their procedural knowledge to creating correct Target Language examples in context.

Copy the whole verb pattern for each of the five tenses you want to practise onto a PowerPoint slide and then project this onto the board. By verb pattern I mean the endings for all of the subject pronouns for a tense. So, for example, for the present tense in French you would have the complete conjugation of -*er*, -*ir* and -*re* verbs for all six subject pronouns. (Give the students practice at building sentences and paragraphs with the regular verbs first before throwing the irregulars at them.) Cram all of these onto one (or two) slide(s). Otherwise, give students a handout with them on.

Take about ten minutes to get the students practising the verb endings of the five tenses using VFLAs or some other means. Then the students get into groups of four. Give each pair of students in the four a handout on which they can write the Target Language for each tense in one column and then the English translation in the column next to it. This is the Five-Tense Blaster document:

Tense name	Infinitive	Spanish example in yo *form* German example in ich *form* French example in je/j' *form*	English translation
Present			
Preterite			
Imperfect			
Future			
Conditional			

Each student writes the name of each of the five tenses they have practised in the first column, as in the example above. In the second column, put a different infinitive on each line. Prime each group with a handout containing a list of thirty or forty regular infinitives in the Target Language (no irregular verbs). Each group of four chooses five infinitives from the handout and writes them in the second column.

They might now have this:

Tense name	Infinitive	Spanish example in yo *form* German example in ich *form* French example in je/j' *form*	English translation
Present	*comer*		
Preterite	*hablar*		
Imperfect	*beber*		
Future	*comprar*		
Conditional	*vivir*		

In the third column, the students conjugate each infinitive according to the tense in the first column – just the 'I' form – and then write the equivalent English translation in the third column:

Tense name	Infinitive	Spanish example in yo *form* German example in ich *form* French example in je/j' *form*	English translation
Present	*comer*	*como*	I eat
Preterite	*hablar*	*hablé*	I spoke
Imperfect	*beber*	*bebía*	I was drinking/ I used to drink
Future	*comprar*	*compraré*	I will buy
Conditional	*vivir*	*viviría*	I would live

Once both pairs in each group have completed their Five-Tense Blaster document in a similar way to the above example they then show you. If all the verbs are conjugated correctly with the appropriate English translation then they move on to Stage Two.

In Stage Two the groups use all of the verbs they've conjugated to write a structured paragraph that makes logical and grammatical sense. They can do this with the help of textbooks, dictionaries and any handouts they wish.

Finally, the groups write their paragraph onto the MWB on the wall. Monitor each group's effort and provide appropriate feedback. You may then choose the three best paragraphs and discuss with the class the steps that they have gone through to reach this point.

Preparation and resources

- Identify the five tenses that you want the class to practise. Copy conjugations of regular verbs in each tense onto a PowerPoint slide. (If this doesn't fit onto one slide, then use two slides or prepare a set of handouts for the students.)
- Print off a class set of Five-Tense Blaster documents and a class set of common regular topic infinitives handouts.
- Provide a supply of dictionaries, textbooks and any other useful resources for the students to use.
- Stick up enough MWBs around your classroom for groups of four. Have marker pens available.
- Project the tense endings onto the board.

Instructions

- Tell the class that they will be working in pairs with another pair, and that in this group of four they will work together to produce a paragraph incorporating five tenses.
- Before they do this, spend ten minutes or so using some VFLAs to practise the endings of the tenses projected on the board.
- The students get into pairs, join another pair and find a base.
- Hand out the Five-Tense Blaster documents and common regular topic infinitives handouts, one per pair.
- Each pair works together, writing down the names of the five tenses in column 1, choosing five different infinitives from their handout and putting each into a separate box in column 2 of the Five-Tense Blaster document. Both pairs in each group must choose the same five infinitives.
- In the third column they convert each infinitive into the 'I' form of the tense and write the English translation for each tense in the final column. Model this for the students as above.
- When both pairs have done this, they show it to you. If the conjugations are correct they go on to the next stage; if not then you feed back on how to fix it.

- When a group of four has had its 'I' form tenses and translations approved they get a board pen and move to a MWB where they write a paragraph which connects all five tenses. Tell them that you will judge these paragraphs.

Variations to the FLA

- Vary the number of tenses. It might be that you want students to practise endings for three tenses, then apply the three tenses in a paragraph.
- Give the pairs and (later) give the groups of four roles as with other FLAs; tense endings boss for one student in each pair and scribe for the other. When they come together as a group of four to write the paragraph on the MWB allocate two further roles: dictionary researcher and textbook researcher.

Teacher notes

Instead of just having regular infinitives, add some extra detail. For example, with infinitives such as *comer*, *hablar* and so on, add some small chunks of language – *comer en un restaurante* or *hablar español* – to help them produce a paragraph.

Planning is important in this FLA. Suggest the students take time to consider which infinitives they could use in a combined manner. Once they have generated their five statements, they take five minutes to plan the paragraph they are going to write on the MWB.

By laminating a set of Five-Tense Blaster documents, the students could write on them using marker pens, thus making them re-usable.

36 Dictation Dictation Retranslation (FLA)

This is a lesson-long FLA for the students to practise listening, speaking, reading and writing. It is an extension of Front-to-Front (FLA #24). There are three stages, in which the students retranslate a Target Language piece based on an English paragraph that they have already translated from the Target Language.

Preparation and resources

- Identify the topic that you want students to practise speaking and spelling the language for. Type out two Target Language paragraphs of near identical length and level of difficulty.
- Put each paragraph on its own PowerPoint slide, together with a third slide featuring both paragraphs.
- Arrange your classroom seating plan so that it allows students to work as pairs with one student facing the board and their partner turning their back to it.
- Only project the Target Language paragraphs when the students are front-to-front so that those with their backs to the board can't see them.

Instructions

1. The Dictation Dictation stage

- Project a Target Language paragraph to do with a topic that has been covered recently (let's say the Future Plans topic).
- Student A faces the board and reads out the paragraph to B who has their back to it and cannot see the paragraph. A can repeat the paragraph as many times as B requests.
- B writes down the Target Language for what is said to them by A. B can ask for anything to be repeated and for A to speak more slowly. All requests must be made in the Target Language. However, B cannot ask A to spell any words or phrases.
- A and B have (within reason) as much time as they need to do this. If any pairs finish early, A repeats the paragraph and B listens and checks their language, until all pairs in class have completed this process.
- Once B has a copy of the paragraph the students swap places. Project a different paragraph, and B dictates that to student A.
- When both paragraphs have been copied, project both Target Language paragraphs onto the board and get the students to correct any mistakes in their work. Have a brief discussion with the class about the types of mistakes made and why.

2. The Translation stage

- The students now translate their corrected Target Language paragraphs into English, on a new page. They may use a dictionary, textbook, or ask you as necessary.
- Project the English translations of both paragraphs onto the board and check with the students that they have translated the Target Language into English correctly.

3. The Retranslation stage

- Explain that they are now going to translate their English versions back into the Target Language. If they want more support they may look back at their corrected, dictated Target Language paragraph, but they will have to add a tally mark for every time they do so.
- Finally, discuss with the students how each one did, how easy they found the process and how many times they looked back at their original Target Language paragraphs.
- Get them to tell you the language that they can now recall from their Target Language paragraph and so on.

Variations to the FLA

- Students work in pairs as pair A and pair B. Pair A take turns dictating the paragraph to pair B, who copy it down, and then vice versa. Having pairs helps to take the pressure off individual students during the retranslation stage.
- Make it competitive! Give students a set of counters each during the retranslation stage; every time they have to look back at their original Target Language paragraph they give you a counter. The student with the most counters remaining (and most accurate translation) wins.
- Use sentences instead of a paragraph.
- Instead of using two paragraphs on the same topic, have paragraphs on two different topics.

Teacher notes

Extension tasks are important! When I first did this FLA I noticed that those students who finished their dictations first sat there task-less. Therefore, when giving the instructions, I told them what to do if they finished early: they could check their work, and then start translating the paragraph into English together, before swapping roles.

Because students work at different speeds, you could give those students who are struggling a handout with the English translation or at least some of the sentences translated to help them.

A further stage (which could be done for homework) would be to set the students a task in which they apply what they have learned to another context. So this is not just about testing their recall but testing how they can recall the language and then adapt it.

It sounds obvious, but make sure that students have enough prior knowledge of the topic(s) before running the FLA and enough practice at using the Target Language requests to get the student doing the dictating to speak more slowly, repeat a word, sentence or paragraph, and so on.

37 The Three Amigos (FLA)

Three activities rolled into one big FLA provide a challenge, given the number of processes involved. This rollercoaster of a FLA involves students working in groups and makes demands on their short-term memories as they engage in dictation and translation tasks.

The idea arose from my experience as a trainee teacher observing classes engaged in a Running Dictation. A Running Dictation goes something like this: copy four different paragraphs of Target Language onto separate pieces of card, fold them over to hide the Target Language and stick these pieces of card up around the room. The students, in groups of three or four, send runners to look at the Target Language paragraph on each of the cards, memorise as much as they can, return to base and dictate what they can remember – in the Target Language – to their team member (the scribe). Students may go back and forth to consult a paragraph as often as they want. The winners are the group which either has the first completed version or the most accurate completed version of the four paragraphs on the walls.

The point of a Running Dictation is that students must hold as much language as possible in their short-term memories for the brief period between reading the paragraph and dictating it to their scribe. Although this activity works well, I wondered if another process could be added after a group had completed the dictation so that they could do something else with the paragraphs.

The Three Amigos FLA works as follows. Start with a Running Dictation (the first amigo). Once a group has completed the four paragraphs, they run the Relay (FLA #3, the second amigo), in which they send a runner to you to check the accuracy of each paragraph. Just as with the Relay FLA, if the first paragraph the runner brings to you is perfect then you approve it and send them back to their base. They then bring the next paragraph and so on until all four have been approved. If a paragraph is not accurate you send the runner back to their group and they continue doing a Running Dictation to correct it.

There's more. Once a group has an approved set of paragraphs they then do another Relay (the third amigo – who bears a striking resemblance to the second amigo), this time translating each paragraph into English, which you approve or not as the case may be. The first group to have translated the paragraphs successfully into English are crowned Three Amigos Champions.

Preparation and resources

- Identify the topic that you want to practise with the students. Write four paragraphs on that topic which are of similar length and perceived difficulty. Print each paragraph onto a separate card, fold each one over and stick them around the room.
- Arrange your classroom seating plan so that groups can work facing each other.

Instructions

- The students get into groups of three at a base and assign the following roles: scribe (does all the writing for all three stages), runner one and runner two (do the memorising and dictating during the Running Dictation, and the running during the Relay).
- Explain that the students are going to do three activities, the winners being the first group to complete all three. All activities must be completed in sequence and a group can only move on to the next activity once they have had the previous stage validated.

1. The First Amigo – Running Dictation based on dictating four Target Language paragraphs

- The first activity is a Running Dictation. There are four paragraphs stuck up around the room; each group sends both of their runners to read and memorise as much of these paragraphs as possible before returning to their base to dictate the paragraphs to their scribe who writes them down.
- The runners may go back and forth between the paragraphs as many times as they like but cannot stand in front of the paragraphs and read them out to their scribe. They have to memorise and then dictate.

2. The Second Amigo – Relay based on validating the dictated Target Language paragraphs

- Once a group has a complete set of paragraphs they do the Relay FLA with each paragraph to check its accuracy. Runner one brings the first paragraph to get it checked.

If it's perfect they do the same for paragraph two until all four have been checked. If a paragraph is not correct, the group continues the Running Dictation until it is.

3. The Third Amigo – Relay based on correctly translating the four Target Language paragraphs

- When a group has had its paragraphs checked for accuracy then the final stage is another Relay, this time translating each paragraph into English. The group translates each paragraph and sends it with one of their runners for you to check. If it's perfect, they do the next paragraph; if not, you send them back to work on it until it is correct.
- The first group to complete this last Relay wins The Three Amigos FLA.

Variations to the FLA

- Vary what you use at the Running Dictation stage: instead of Target Language paragraphs have the card showing the steps to follow in order to form a different tense. The runners in each group have to memorise these steps and dictate them to their scribe.
- Instead of paragraphs, use English sentences as part of the Running Dictation which, after being dictated, the scribe and the rest of the group translate into the Target Language.

Teacher notes

Given the number of processes this makes for a lesson-long FLA. However, you could shorten it by reducing the length of the Target Language paragraphs. Also, during the Running Dictation stage, you could introduce a time limit for the length of time students can stand and memorise the paragraphs.

38 Learning–Mat Builder (FLA)

The Learning-Mat Builder FLA gets the students to reflect on the language they have learned during the previous half-term. It necessitates students having a certain amount of prior language knowledge. This FLA is also a way of practising retrieval of language that has been covered over several weeks.

A Learning Mat is simply a document packed full of key terms, vocabulary, tenses, and so on. A colleague once described them as 'busy', because as much language as possible, related to a particular topic or requirement, is crammed onto an A4 handout.

Project a copy of the Scheme of Learning which has been covered during the previous half-term, but first remove the actual Target Language examples. Just leave the references to the language topics and the names of the tenses.

Conduct a Learning Reminiscence in which you remind the students of each section on the Scheme of Learning. As you do this, ask them to recall the language from the topics and grammar points mentioned. Discuss which areas of the Scheme of Learning they remember learning about and why, which they enjoyed learning and why, and which they did not enjoy learning and why. As you and the class explore these things, you all write down some of the Target Language that you recall arising from the discussion.

Suppose Holidays had been one topic covered during the half-term. Your Scheme of Learning might start with Describing the Weather. Ask the students how many weather terms they can remember, and to make a note of these. There would be insufficient time to record *all* of the language covered in every lesson – and in any case the point of this part of the FLA is to aid recall and make connections between the students' recent learning and the language they learned earlier in the year.

Once you have completed this discussion and the students have made some notes of the Target Language, it's time to get down to the real business of this FLA: the students produce their own Learning Mat based on the language you have just discussed. They can be as creative as they like in making it, so long as it includes all of the topics covered during the half-term and some of the Target Language for each topic. To help with this, give them a textbook and list the appropriate page references for the topics and grammar covered.

That's pretty much it. However, as with many of the FLAs, there is a competitive element. Once students have completed their mats they present them to the class, who judge the three best ones. If there is not much time left, this can be saved for the following lesson.

Preparation and resources

- Identify the relevant section of the Scheme of Learning you want to use. Copy this part of it onto a PowerPoint slide, using English only.
- Get a set of textbooks ready for the students to use.
- Project the Scheme of Learning onto the board so that every student can see it.

Instructions

- Explain that together you are going to revise what has been covered over the last half-term, using the extract from the Scheme of Learning projected on the board as a prompt.
- You will spend fifteen minutes discussing this section of the Scheme of Learning with them and you are all going to write down some of the Target Language for the topics covered as a way of revising.
- After that, the students produce their own Learning Mat. If a class is unfamiliar with the Learning Mat concept, show them some examples.
- The mat should include all of the topics and as much language as possible, presented in a creative way.
- Once students have finished their Learning Mats – if there is enough time in this lesson – they present them to the others. If not, do this the following lesson.

Variations to the FLA

- Run the FLA at the end of each half-term as a way of testing students' retrieval. By doing it every half-term you are effectively adopting spaced practice.
- Get the students to interact with their mats: each student goes and presents their mat to another student for thirty seconds, and then listens and watches another student presenting their mat to them for thirty seconds. Both students note down something that they learned from the other's mat before moving on to do the same with another student.
- Vary the length of the section of the Scheme of Learning that you choose. Instead of half a term, base it over a full term or just two weeks of a Scheme of Learning.

Teacher notes

You could use this FLA with a brand-new class at the start of the year as a way of assessing their prior language knowledge. This would be similar to the Concept Map Activity as referred to in *How Learning Works*, in which the authors suggest that students write down all they know about a particular topic so that you can easily assess their knowledge.[33]

This might be a bit tricky to do with a class who don't have a lot of language to recall, so instead try it as a way of addressing any pre-conceived cultural stereotypes of a country. Present them with a question such as, 'When you think of Spain/France/Germany what do you think of?'

This FLA can also be a good rapport builder because you are recalling shared memories. Reflecting on what has been covered can lead to prompts and reminders like, 'Remember that lesson when x said … ?'

---

[33] Ambrose et al., (2010) p. 30.

39 Progress Gallery (FLA)

The Progress Gallery FLA is an example of modelling progression to GCSE students, and about demonstrating progress.

The idea for this FLA was reinforced by reading the following section of a download from the Specialist Schools and Academies Trust (SSAT) in particular the stated view on what Ofsted inspectors are looking for:

> *What other evidence is there of the progress they have made with you over time? How well do you adapt your teaching to respond to developments during the lesson? (Or do you stick to your lesson plan, come what may?) How well do you challenge your pupils? What is the quality of your assessment and feedback both during the lesson and as shown in exercise books?*[34]

Remember that Ofsted aren't looking for a specific teaching style. The SSAT document also discusses this with reference to Her Majesty's Chief Inspector (HMCI) of Education, Sir Michael Wilshaw's speech to the Royal Society of Arts, in which he said, 'We want to see teaching designed to ensure that children are learning and making progress. After all, that is what good teachers do naturally every day.'[35]

---

[34] SSAT, (2014) 'Ofsted, Outstanding Teaching and TEEP'. p. 2. See http://www.ssatuk.co.uk/wp-content/uploads/2013/11/Ofsted-Outstanding-Teaching-and-TEEPFebruary-2014.pdf.

[35] Michael Wilshaw, (2012) 'The Good Teacher' (speech) transcribed in RSA digital journal. See http://www.thersa.org/fellowship/journal/archive/summer-2012/features/the-good-teacher.

The key message here is that you need to measure and have evidence of the progress students are making. However, first comes the teaching. If we want students to make exceptional progress then as teacher experts we model the stages we want the student novices to go through to get to that position. Students need to know what exceptional progress is if they are going to achieve it.

You may have seen or even used a display of pieces of work shown in ascending order of the grade they would get (or did get, if the pieces have been marked). You are going to create an example of this.

Prepare a basic piece of written work (a couple of sentences). This is the first document. Copy this onto a second document and add one or two more sentences to improve it. Continue doing this with a third, fourth, fifth and sixth document, with this final document being an A* piece of writing (or a 9 following the changes in GCSE grading).[36] Annotate each document to show what has been done at every stage to improve it, thus showing the progress.

There are several ways of presenting the Progress Gallery to students. I've stuck up six MWBs across the back of the classroom and written my pieces with a marker pen, starting with the most basic version on the first board, a slightly improved version on the next, and so on until the sixth board has the A*/9 version. As I talk through why one piece is better than another, I get some student volunteers to annotate my written pieces on the boards.

A more high-tech Progress Gallery (which sits somewhere between the traditional marker pen/board method and the students using iPads, iPhones and the like) uses a ShowMe app.[37] I use Microsoft Photo Story 3 for Windows to project a photo and record a commentary on the features of each piece of writing. Using Photo Story to create digital stories is well described in *Distance Learning … For Educators, Trainers, and Leaders* and for the purposes of the instructions below I will assume a knowledge of how to work it (I'll use the 'If I can use it then anyone can' line now).[38]

Using Photo Story means taking a digital photo of each of the six progress documents, putting them into Photo Story in order and then recording a commentary describing the progression features of each document. Students thus get to see the incremental improvements from the most basic to the most advanced piece of writing – and that's your Progress Gallery on display. You might want students to note two techniques that they have learned from each photo and its commentary.

---

[36] See http://www.aqa.org.uk/news-and-policy/policy/gcse-and-a-level-changes/structure-of-new-gcses.

[37] See http://www.showme.com.

[38] Duysevi Karan-Miyar, (2009) 'Digital Storytelling: Using Photo Story 3 to Create Digital Stories', *Distance Learning … For Educators, Trainers, and Leaders* (6) 1, 27–29.

However, it's all well and good modelling progress in this way, but can you get the students to apply what they have learned to another context? You bet you can. Create another Photo Story showing progression features with a set of similar Target Language written work pieces but without the commentary. The students then write an English commentary on the improvements made to these pieces.

Preparation and resources

- Put six progressive examples on separate pages, starting with a basic piece of written work, followed by a slightly improved version, and so on until the sixth piece is the very best quality of writing that you would expect from the students.
- Scan each document or take a photo using a digital camera. Put these six images in sequence into Photo Story to show the sequence of improvement. Have the image for each piece of work remain visible for between thirty seconds and one minute.
- Add a commentary for each image on Photo Story, describing the features of each piece and what has been done to improve it. Save the Photo Story.
- Set up the Photo Story ready to play on the board to the students.

Instructions

- Explain to the class that you are going to show a Photo Story of a piece of work at several stages of improvement. Each stage lasts a minute and has an added commentary describing the changes.
- The students note down two techniques (or vocabulary, short phrases, features and so on) about each photo and its commentary. They will feed these back to you afterwards.
- Play the Photo Story. Discuss with the students the features of each piece and which techniques they noted down and why.

Variations to the FLA

- You could project stages of an annotated mark scheme, previous students' work (getting their permission first!), GCSE marked exemplars and so on to make a graded Progress Gallery.
- Reverse the process: make a Photo Story showing the very best piece first, then a less developed piece and so on.

- Get the students to create their own Progress Gallery of their writing skills over the term. Keep the pieces in class and every time a student has learned a new piece of language they add to it (for instance, using adjectives with nouns or how to incorporate the Target Language for conjunctions such as *where* or *when* to extend sentences in their writing).
- Extend the FLA to include an application phase where students make their own commentary on a Progress Gallery (as suggested in the introduction).

Teacher notes

As with Teacher vs. YouTube (FLA #6) you could actually use the clip that you are going to play for the students as a Scene-Setter (FLA #40) and have it playing as soon as students enter the classroom to provoke curiosity.

40 Scene–Setters (FLA)

I've grouped together a number of ideas that I've used and observed other teachers using as, dare I say it, starters. So how about AFKAS – Activities Formerly Known As Starters. Some of these AFKAS were inspired by different initiatives and/or teachers.

The following FLAs are based on scene-setting to ensure that the learning environment is set up as the students come into the classroom. They establish the learning mood from the off.

1. Project onto the board a table with the letters A–Z down the left-hand side with space to the right. As the students enter, call out the name of a topic, such as Healthy Living, and the students get into pairs and write as many Target Language words as they can to do with Healthy Living, each beginning with a different letter. They can use textbooks and dictionaries alongside their own memories. The first pair to get 20 words wins (in some Target Languages it would be extremely difficult to complete the alphabet).
2. The classic odd-one-out. When the students enter the classroom you already have five different groups of Target Language words projected onto the board, each group containing a word that is an odd-one-out. The students sit down, find the odd-one-out and write a sentence in Target Language or English explaining why they think that. (You could also do something similar with the ubiquitous Target Language anagrams.)
3. Play music or a YouTube clip that relates in some way to the content of the lesson or the topic you're about to cover. For example, if you're about to start the Holidays topic, play Madonna's 'Holiday' as students come into class (if you can find a Target Language version of it even better!).

Many films have versions dubbed in various languages. You could play part of a DVD which has a soundtrack in the Target Language, or find a clip on YouTube. For example, for the topic of Food, try the opening of the Spanish version of *Ratatouille*, which will get the students in the right frame of mind for learning food and drink vocabulary or how to order in a restaurant.[39]

Preparation and resources

- For an AFKAS which is an Odd-One-Out, Anagram or Mistakes In A Sentence, identify the Target Language you want students to practise, put it on a PowerPoint slide and project it onto the board. With A–Z create a two-column table with the alphabet in the left-hand column and space in the right-hand column for the students to write words beginning with each letter.
- With a DVD or YouTube clip, find the section of the DVD or the clip on YouTube and set it up ready to play as soon as the students are coming into class.

Instructions

- With Odd-One-Out, tell the students as they arrive that they need to look at the groups of Target Language words, choose the odd-one-out and justify their reasoning. Tell them whether to write their justification in English or in the Target Language.
- With Anagrams, tell the students that they have five minutes to write the Target Language words for the anagrams on the board. The first student to do this wins.
- With A–Z, tell the students to get into pairs with one student as the dictionary researcher and the other as the scribe. The dictionary researcher has to find a Target Language word beginning with a different letter of the alphabet and the scribe writes the word down. All the words must relate to the topic and must be in the Target Language, whether they're nouns, verbs, adjectives and so on. The first pair to find a list of twenty A–Z Target Language words wins.

Variations to the FLA

- Project an image or photo on any topic and as the students come in tell them they have to use a dictionary to find twenty Target Language words relating to the picture. The first group to compile twenty and show you wins.

---

[39] See https://www.youtube.com/watch?v=oj1s8xiO8Xo.

- Have the instructions for what to do already written up on the board so all you have to do when the students enter the classroom is to point at the board. This saves you having to repeat instructions for latecomers.
- Use the clips from YouTube at the end of a lesson as a sneak preview of what will be in store for the next lesson. Don't tell them what the topic is though, just show the clip. Have a competition and challenge them to work out what the topic will be. When you see the students in and around school before the following lesson ask them if they have worked out what it is – a great rapport builder.
- There are many other types of Scene-Setters: as soon as the students enter the room, have a Prezi (a sort of virtual presentation) running, showing a presentation of an imaginary character's life (their personal details such as brothers and sisters, school routine and so on). Tell them that they have to write five Target Language words from the Prezi that they don't know the meaning of and look these up in the dictionary.
- You could have a PowerPoint slide up on the board with a set of QR codes on it and as soon as students enter class they have to read the codes with their phones (if your school policy allows this) or iPads (if you're lucky enough to have a set). Students read the QR codes and each code takes them to complete a different task; the first student to complete the tasks wins.

Teacher notes

The Scene-Setters FLA could be a list of various activities that you use not just to start the lesson off in the way that you want it, but as a way of setting up students' learning over several lessons to come. You could use a YouTube clip to foreshadow what the students will be learning over the next half or whole term.

Chapter 6

Exemplars of VFLAs and FLAs and Spaced Practice

Hattie's research in *Visible Learning* shows spaced versus massed practice to have a powerful effect size of d = 0.71. Hattie refers to Nuthall, who, as Hattie puts it, 'claimed that students often needed three to four exposures to the learning – usually over several days – before there was a reasonable probability that they would learn.'[1]

Given the benefits of spaced practice as described above and elsewhere in this book, I've put together two examples of the VFLAs and FLAs in context. Below are two tables: the first details a two-week plan and the second a half-term plan showing how you could use the VFLAs and FLAs together to achieve a particular learning result over that time period.

---

1 Hattie, (2009) p. 186.

These plans are based on my own experience. They are characterised by spaced practice of the language that I want the students to know by the end. Both plans are based on a two-week timetable of four hour-long lessons over the two weeks; two lessons per week. As Ernesto Macaro refers to in *Debates In Modern Languages,* the average amount of curriculum time given over to learning languages for students aged 11 to 16 in the UK is two hours a week.[2]

The first plan, which illustrates how the VFLAs, FLAs and spaced practice could be used over a two-week period, is broken down per lesson over the fortnight. I decided not to include timings because this might suggest a greater focus on the length of the activity rather than allowing for flexibility.

The second plan describes how the VFLAs, FLAs and spaced practice could be used over a half-term period. It is broken down per week of the half-term. I have numbered the suggested activities, which are designed to show progression inclusive of spaced practice.

I must emphasise that neither plan is meant to be prescriptive, just illustrative of how spaced practice of vocabulary and tense formation could take place.

It is assumed, of course, that the same set of thirty to forty words of key vocabulary (for the first plan) and Free Time vocabulary (for the second plan) would be used.

I have highlighted the spaced practice of vocabulary in bold and left the spaced practice of tenses as they are since the FLAs used in each lesson will involve the students practising the tenses.

---

[2] Macaro in Driscoll et al., (2014) p. 118.

Example one:
Year 9 GCSE class based on a two-week plan

Learning result: students are able to use two new tenses in sentences and know the meaning of at least twenty words of key vocabulary by the end of the two-week plan.

Week One

Day	Lesson
Monday	1. Direct instruction of key vocab, then VFLAs and test retrieval. 2. Direct instruction and feedback on present tense. 3. To The Walls FLA students practise conjugating whole paradigm of all three infinitives in present tense. 4. Task Corner FLA students write an infinitive for another student in class to conjugate in the present tense for a lesson next week.
Tuesday	No lesson.
Wednesday	1. Scene-Setters FLA students choose odd-one-out from group of present tense endings. 2. VFLAs with present tense verb endings. 3. Direct instruction and feedback on revision of present tense and how to use it to build paragraphs. Teach present tense time phrases and connectives. Examples in books. 4. Relay FLA students translate English sentences into present tense. 5. **Spaced practice of key vocab and test retrieval.**
Thursday	No lesson.
Friday	No lesson.

Week Two

Day	*Lesson*
Monday	1. Task Corner FLA students complete their sticky note task on MWB. 2. **Spaced practice of key vocab and test retrieval.** 3. To The Walls FLA students build present tense paragraphs with time phrases and connectives. 4. Direct instruction and feedback on future tense. 5. Project A Board Game FLA: endings of the future tense.
Tuesday	No lesson.
Wednesday	No lesson.
Thursday	No lesson.
Friday	1. **Spaced practice of key vocab and test retrieval**. 2. Direct instruction and feedback on revision of future tense and how to use it to build paragraphs. Teach future tense time phrases and connectives. Examples in books. 3. Statement Stand-Up FLA: statements in both tenses. 4. Direct instruction and feedback on combining present tense and future tense. Examples in books. 5. To The Walls FLA students demonstrate they can write a paragraph with two tenses by writing on MWB and sign their names to prove their progress. 6. **Test retrieval of key vocab.**

Example two:
Year 8 class based on a half-term plan

Learning result: students are able to use three new tenses in a paragraph about Free Time and recognise at least thirty words of key vocabulary by the end of the half-term plan.

Week on timetable	Brief lesson summary of the week
Week 1	1. Scheme of Learning Trailer FLA.
	2. Direct instruction to teach Free Time vocab.
	3. VFLAs with Free Time vocab.
	4. Seeing Double FLA with present tense.
	5. Direct instruction of how to use the present tense with time phrases and connectives.
	6. Write, Pass, Read, Write, Pass FLA with present tense, time phrases and connectives.
Week 2	7. **Spaced practice of Free Time vocabulary with VFLAs.**
	8. Teacher modelling of how to write Free Time present tense paragraph.
	9. To The Walls FLA with students writing a paragraph about their Free Time.
	10. Students write Free Time present tense paragraph in books.
	11. Stand Up Sit Down FLA with present tense and past tense.
Week 1	12. **Spaced practice of Free Time vocabulary with VFLAs and test retrieval.**
	13. Direct instruction of how to use the past tense with time phrases and connectives.
	14. Pull The Switch FLA with past tense dialogue.
	15. Direct instruction of present tense and past tense combined.
	16. Task Corner FLA with task on writing with two tenses.
	17. Reading and listening work on Free Time.
Week 2	18. **Spaced practice of Free Time vocabulary with VFLAs and test retrieval.**
	19. Painting The Preterite Tense FLA with students using the present tense or the preterite tense.
	20. Student practice using present and past tense in a paragraph.
	21. Direct instruction of how to use the future tense with time phrases and connectives.
	22. Back-to-Front FLA with sentences in past, present and future tenses.

Week 1	23. Before, Now, After and Forever FLA with students practising the past, present and future tenses.
	24. Reading and listening work on Free Time with texts containing three tenses.
	25. **Spaced practice of Free Time vocabulary with VFLAs and test retrieval.**
	26. Task Corner FLA with task on writing with two tenses.
	27. Task Corner FLA with task on writing with three tenses.
	28. **Spaced practice of Free Time vocabulary with VFLAs and test retrieval.**
	29. Direct instruction of how to use the present, past and future tenses with time phrases and connectives.
Week 2	30. Student practice using present, past and future tense in a paragraph with time phrases and connectives.
	31. Relay FLA with all three tenses.
	32. To The Walls FLA with students writing a paragraph about their Free Time using three tenses.
	33. **Spaced practice of Free Time vocabulary with VFLAs and test retrieval.**
	34. Reading and listening work on Free Time with texts containing three tenses.
	35. Task Corner FLA with task on writing with three tenses.
	36. Student assessment on writing about Free Time using three tenses.
	37. **Spaced practice of Free Time vocabulary with VFLAs and test retrieval.**

Chapter 7

Maxims

Here are some maxims that I follow, and I want to share them because they have worked for me. They're not intended to be prescriptive commands, rather a selection of approaches and rules, some of which you might want to trial.

1. Be flexible: don't be tied to teaching a word just because the Scheme of Learning says you have to teach it then. Plan your teaching around students' learning needs and not what you need to get taught.
2. Include enough time, no matter what language topic the students are studying, to include spaced practice of key, long-term-memory-essential knowledge in lessons.
3. Develop and deliver as many different, fun, interesting and exciting learning strategies and activities as possible that mirror the knowledge and skills that the students will need in order to make outstanding progress in their exams.

4. Design and deliver assessments which mirror how students will be assessed in their exams. Get the students practising early.
5. Do spaced practice with past papers as early as possible – don't leave them until towards the end of the course.
6. Talk to the students about *why* you are doing an activity. 'Sell the rationale' to the students and be positive.
7. Refer to the VFLAs and FLAs by name with the students to help to create rapport with a class.
8. During the lesson, adapt to the pace of students' learning and not the pace at which you get activities done with a class.
9. Spend time planning lessons rather than planning lesson plans.
10. Put yourself in the students' position of knowledge: before teaching anything ask yourself what language knowledge they need to know in order to make progress.

Chapter 8

Taking This Further

VFLAs with other subjects

There is more to education than learning modern foreign languages. It is perfectly possible to adapt the activities I have developed – the VFLAs and FLAs – for use in practising other kinds of knowledge across the curriculum. There is always 'stuff that students need to know' upon which they build their understanding. It's essential they can recall underpinning knowledge from their long-term memories when faced with solving problems which take up the majority of their working memory.

The VFLAs can be used in a similar way to their role in language learning: to target key, exam-related knowledge – the type of stuff that students just need to have readily available. Every subject has a basic set of core facts that the students need to know and then apply to solve problems. The generic process is:

1. The teacher identifies the most important knowledge for the students to be successful in their exams and imparts this knowledge.
2. The students learn and practise the knowledge using VFLAs.
3. The teacher tests retrieval.
4. The students demonstrate their understanding by applying this knowledge in other contexts to solve novel problems.

Take geography, for example. I scanned several past exam papers, looking for questions which required students to recall something from their long-term memories in order to answer them and to apply this knowledge to another problem. Unsurprisingly, I found many examples of this. For instance, the AQA Higher (Specification A) Unit 2 Human Geography paper has the following task to complete:

> *2 (b) (i) Describe disadvantages of building new housing on brownfield sites. Use **Figure 5** and your own knowledge.*[1]

So let's suppose you listed all the disadvantages, put them up on the board and then ran some VFLAs as you would do with vocabulary and short phrases.

A great deal of information, facts about curriculum content, has already been sorted, listed, and converted into bullet points and is available online and in Pass Notes type books. This material covers the basics for getting into a subject; you need to know this first before you can start exploring in depth. So what's to stop the teacher typing this fundamental stuff onto PowerPoint slides and getting the students to familiarise themselves with it using VFLAs?

The difference with MFL is that nearly all the content has to be learned this way. With other curriculum subjects, the students come with prior knowledge – after all, they've been absorbing information about their culture, the world they live in, for several years already. Then, armed with more facts from the Scheme of Learning, they are ready to apply and generalise this knowledge to use in unfamiliar contexts; to examine, understand and solve the problems that each curriculum subject poses. The more they have consolidated the basics, the better they will be able to do this.

---

[1] See http://filestore.aqa.org.uk/subjects/AQA-40302H-QP-JUN13.pdf.

Conclusion

As I mentioned at the beginning of Chapter 6, the average amount of curriculum time given over to learning languages for students aged 11 to 16 in the UK is two hours a week. This is not a lot of time for teenagers to create automaticity and fluency in a MFL. The activities I have described here make this challenge more feasible.

I don't expect every teacher to follow every activity to the letter. That's not what they are about. I have described my progress in creating these activities in the hope that it will inspire you to adopt and adapt them to suit your personality and the classes you teach.

The essential thing is that they are fun for you to do. That's what really counts. You are creating a classroom atmosphere where learning becomes enjoyable, and thus more effective.

Acknowledgments

The biggest *gracias*, *danke* and *merci* has to go to David Bowman at Crown House and Caroline Lenton, formerly at Crown House, and equally to my editor, Peter Young. The support I have had from them has been amazing, especially given that they had to endure my first version written in Comic Sans MS font … Rosalie Williams and Bev Randell at Crown House have also been a huge support and thanks to them.

I have to also thank my partner Emily for support and inspiration, especially while I was living in the office at home; my mum and brother (and his wife) for providing teaching and learning inspiration and to my dad, who has passed judgment on excerpts I have sent him.

Finally, thanks to the fantastic, hard-working staff and students in the three wonderful schools that I have worked in: Alsager School, Arthur Terry School and Heart of England School.

Bibliography

Ahour, T., Pajoman, N. and Tamjid, N. H. (2013) 'The Effect of Vocabulary Flooding Technique on Iranian EFL Elementary Learners' Vocabulary Learning', *International Journal of Applied Linguistics & English Literature*, Vol. 2 No. 6; November. pp. 185–193. See http://www.academia.edu/5329417/The-effect-of-vocabulary-flooding-on-Iranian-EFL-elementarylearners-vocabulary-learning.

Ambrose, S. A., Bridges, M. W., DiPietro, M., Lovett, M. C., Norman, M. K. and Mayer, R. E. (2010) *How Learning Works: Seven Research-Based Principles for Smart Teaching*, San Francisco, Jossey-Bass.

Barton, A. (2006) *Getting the Buggers Into Languages*, London, Bloomsbury Education.

Beadle, P. (2010) *How to Teach*, Carmarthen, Crown House Publishing.

Beere, J. (2012) *The Perfect Ofsted Lesson*, Carmarthen, Independent Thinking Press.

Bennett, T. (2013) *Teacher Proof: Why Research in Education Doesn't Always Mean What it Claims, and What You Can Do About it*, Abingdon, Routledge.

Blackburn, B. (2007) *Classroom Instruction from A to Z*, Abingdon, Routledge.

Brookhart, S. M. (2008) *How to Give Effective Feedback to Your Students*, Association for Supervision & Curriculum Development.

Brophy, J. (2004) *Motivating Students to Learn*, Abingdon, Routledge.

Brown, P. C., Roediger III, H. L. and McDaniel, M. A. (2014) *Make It Stick: The Science of Successful Learning*, Cambridge, MA, Harvard University Press.

Buttner, A. (2007) *Activities, Games, Assessment Strategies, and Rubrics For The Foreign Language Classroom*, Abingdon, Routledge.

Carey, B. (2014) *How We Learn: The Surprising Truth about When, Where and Why it Happens*, London, Macmillan.

Didau, D. (2014) *The Secret of Literacy: Making the Implicit, Explicit*, Carmarthen, Independent Thinking Press.

Didau, D. (2013) 'The Problem with Fun', *Learning Spy* (blog). See http://www.learningspy.co.uk/education/the-problem-with-fun/.

Driscoll, P., Macaro, E. and Swarbrick, A. (Eds) (2014) *Debates in Modern Languages Education*, Abingdon, Routledge.

Dweck, C. S. (2012) *Mindset: How You Can Fulfil Your Potential*, London, Constable & Robinson.

Francis, S. (2003) 'Input Flooding and the Acquisition of the Spanish Verbs Ser and Estar for Beginning-Level Adult Learners', PhD thesis, Purdue University, Lafayette, IN. See http://docs.lib.purdue.edu/dissertations/AAI3113799/.

Ginnis, P. (2002) *The Teacher's Toolkit: Raise Classroom Achievement with Strategies for Every Learner*, Carmarthen, Crown House Publishing.

Graves, M. F. (2006) *The Vocabulary Book: Learning & Instruction*, New York, Teachers College Press.

Griffith, A. and Burns, M. (2012) *Outstanding Teaching: Engaging Learners*, Carmarthen, Crown House Publishing.

Hattie, J. (2009) *Visible Learning: A Synthesis of Over 800 Meta-Analyses Relating to Achievement*, Abingdon, Routledge.

Hattie, J. (2012) *Visible Learning For Teachers: Maximizing Impact on Learning*, Abingdon, Routledge.

Jones, J. and Wiliam, D. (2008) *Modern Foreign Languages: Inside the Black Box*, Chiswick, GL Assessment.

Karan-Miyar, D. (2009) 'Digital Storytelling: Using Photo Story 3 to Create Digital Stories', *Distance Learning … For Educators, Trainers, and Leaders*, (6) 1, 27–29.

Knight, O. and Benson, D. (2014) *Creating Outstanding Classrooms: A Whole-School Approach*, Abingdon, Routledge.

Lemov, D. (2010) *Teach Like a Champion: 49 Techniques That Put Students on the Path to College*, San Francisco, Jossey-Bass.

Lemov, D., Woolway, E. and Yezzi, K. (2012) *Practice Perfect: 42 Rules for Getting Better at Getting Better*, San Francisco, Jossey-Bass.

Major, M. R. (2008) *The Teacher's Survival Guide: Real Classroom Dilemmas and Practical Solutions*, Lanham, MD, Rowman & Littlefield Education.

Mangen, A. and Velay, J.-L. (2010) 'Digitizing Literacy: Reflections on the Haptics of Writing', in Mehrdad Hosseini Zadeh (Ed.) *Advances in Haptics*, InTech, DOI: 10.5772/8710. Available from: http://www.intechopen.com/books/advances-in-haptics/digitizing-literacy-reflections-on-the-haptics-of-writing.

McGill, R. M. (2013) *100 Ideas for Secondary Teachers: Outstanding Lessons*, London, Bloomsbury Education.

Nevid, Jeff (2011) 'Teaching the Millennials', *(Association for Psychological Science) Observer* Vol. 24, No. 5 May/June.

Ofsted (2015) *School Inspection Handbook*. Ref: 120101. Available at http://www.gov.uk/government/publications/school-inspection-handbook.

Ofsted (2014) *Inspection Report: Fernhill School*, 20–21 March. See http://www.ofsted.gov.uk/inspection-reports/find-inspection-report/provider/ELS/116447.

Ofsted (2013) *Inspection Report: Heart of England School*, 13–14 November. Sec http://www.ofsted.gov.uk/inspection-reports/find-inspection-report/provider/ELS/136909.

Old, A. (2010) 'The Outstanding School', *Scenes From The Battleground* (blog). See https://teachingbattleground.wordpress.com/2010/11/22/the-outstanding-school/.

Parker Palmer, J. (2007) *The Courage to Teach: Exploring the Inner Landscape of a Teacher's Life*, San Francisco, Jossey-Bass.

Peal, R. (2014) *Progressively Worse: The Burden of Bad Ideas in British Schools*, London, Civitas.

Petty, G. (2009) *Evidence-Based Teaching*, 2nd edition, Cheltenham, Nelson Thornes.

Pimsleur, P. (1967) 'A Memory Schedule', *Modern Language Journal* (51: 75).

SSAT (2014) 'Ofsted, Outstanding Teaching and TEEP'. See http://www.ssatuk.co.uk/wp-content/uploads/ 2013/11/Ofsted-Outstanding-Teaching-and-TEEPFebruary-2014.pdf.

Stahl, S. A. (1999) *Vocabulary Development*, Brookline, MA, Brookline Books.

Takač, V. P. (2008) *Vocabulary Learning Strategies and Foreign Language Acquisition*, Clevedon, Multilingual Matters Ltd.

Wells, J. (1996) 'Why Phonetic Transcription is Important', *Journal of the Phonetic Society of Korea*, No. 31–32:239–242, December. See http://www.phon.ucl.ac.uk/home/wells/whytranscription.htm.

Willingham, D. T. (2009) *Why Don't Students Like School?*, San Francisco, Jossey-Bass.

Index

Available for Download
www.crownhouse.co.uk/featured/fun-mfl

Here are the filenames of the resources from the book to get you started in your classroom.

Here are the filenames of the postcard illustrations from the book for you to use in your classroom.

Page 23	French
Page 28	Spanish
Page 37	Spanish
Page 41	French
Page 45	German
Page 48	German
Page 52	Spanish
Page 56	French
Page 60	German
Page 64	Spanish
Page 67	French
Page 71	German
Page 75	Spanish
Page 79	French
Page 83	German
Page 87	Spanish
Page 90	French
Page 93	German
Page 96	Spanish
Page 100	French
Page 124	Spanish
Page 135	French
Page 154	French
Page 157	French
Page 161	German
Page 203	Spanish
Page 204	Spanish
Page 212	Five-Tense Blaster

French costume postcard
French food postcard
French landmark postcard
German costume postcard
German food postcard
German landmark postcard
Spanish food postcard
Spanish costume postcard
Spanish landmark postcard

Exam Literacy

A guide to doing what works (and not what doesn't) to better prepare students for exams

Jake Hunton

ISBN: 978-178583198-0

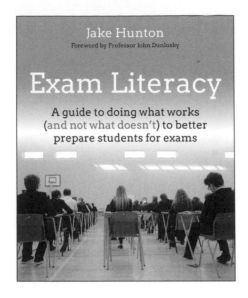

In Exam Literacy Jake Hunton focuses on the latest cognitive research into revision techniques and delivers proven strategies which actually work.

In this wide-ranging guide to effective exam preparation, Jake Hunton casts a careful eye over a wide range of research into revision techniques and details the strategies which have been proven to deliver the best results. With plenty of practical suggestions and subject-specific examples, *Exam Literacy* provides teachers with user-friendly advice on how they can make the content they cover stick, and shares up-to-date, evidence-based information on:

- The nature of learning and the various types of memory.
- How to improve students' retention of knowledge and recall of content.
- Why popular revision techniques, such as rereading, highlighting and summarising, may not be as effective as you think.
- How revision strategies that have been identified as being more effective – such as interleaving, elaborative interrogation, self-explanation and retrieval practice – can be embedded into day-to-day teaching.
- How students can be encouraged to make use of these winning strategies when revising independently.

The book also shows how the proven revision strategies which Jake details could work alongside subject content, and explores the overlap between the use of revision strategies in and out the classroom – suggesting ways to fill any learning gaps. As an additional focus, Jake discusses why teachers may be better off delivering their own revision (or 'revisiting') strategies as part of the normal flow of their teaching of the curriculum rather than resorting to after-school revision sessions or outsourcing to revision companies.

Suitable for all teachers looking to improve their students' exam results.